Gardens to Go

Gardens to Go

Creating and Designing
a Container Garden

Sydney Eddison

Photography by Steve Silk

Bulfinch Press

New York • Boston

Bulfinch Press

Time Warner Book Group

1271 Avenue of the Americas, New York, NY 10020

Visit our Web site at www.bulfinchpress.com

First Edition

Library of Congress Cataloging-in-Publication Data

Eddison, Sydney.

Gardens to go : creating and designing a container garden / Sydney Eddison.—1st ed.

p. cm.

Includes index.

ISBN 0-8212-5715-3

1. Container gardening.   I. Title.

SB418.E33 2005

635.9'86—dc22   2004020125

Design by Kay Schuckhart/Blond on Pond

PRINTED IN SINGAPORE

In memory of my friends
Hartney Arthur (1917–2004) and
Markland Taylor (1936–2003)

Contents

For *the* Fun *of* It

During the last six years, I've made a different container garden on the terrace every summer. And I've never had more fun. Incidentally, making a container garden is not the same thing as using potted plants for decoration. Decoration is intended to be looked at; a garden, even if it is grown in pots, is meant to be experienced.

In terms of design, a container garden should have boundaries, bone structure, and geometry, just like any other garden. If the basic shape is rectilinear, there will be corners that must be addressed; if curving, the ends and edges will require definition. As most patios, decks, and terraces are attached or closely allied to homes and buildings, it makes sense to treat these out-

door spaces as if they were rooms and to provide a sense of enclosure.

Within the enclosure, there should be variety, repetition, and centers of interest, all of which can be achieved with groups of potted plants. Combined with a few simple props, like trellises, obelisks, columns, and plant stands, plants in containers can create walls, direct traffic, screen out undesirable sights, frame appealing views, and supply focal points.

The reason this kind of gardening appeals to me so much is that it is just like stage design, especially in summer stock, where the trick is to come up with a different set every week, on a shoestring and on the double. In my day, we used to raise the curtain every Monday night on a whole new world by reconfiguring wall units, shuffling around props, and slapping on a fresh coat of paint. A little sleight of hand, and voilà! Another opening of another show! That's what I loved about summer stock. And that's what I love about container gardens. Instant gratification — almost — and something new to look at every year.

In *Gardens to Go*, you will meet a total of eight container gardeners, including my partner, photographer Steve Silk, and me. Those of us who indulge this delicious pastime are passionate in its pursuit. Although we are still few in number, what we do is something that anybody can do, almost anywhere, and get enormous pleasure from it. Moreover, I believe that this kind of small-scale garden making is the wave of the future.

As you will soon see, a container garden is the real thing, a living three-dimensional picture, rich in plant material and every bit as exciting as an in-the-ground garden. If you already garden on terra firma, you will find many of the steps the same, but much less arduous. Essentially, all gardens are made in the same way, whether they are in the ground or elsewhere. There is a logical progression from whim to execution that involves learning about the site, discovering which plants belong there, experimenting with their arrangement, and figuring out how to maintain your creation once it is in place. *Gardens to Go* proceeds along just these lines, starting with first things first.

If you have never made a container garden before, the gardeners in this book are ready to help you. If you are an old hand at container gardening, you will meet new friends who share your passion. Steve and I are both obsessed container gardeners. We have also collaborated before and, in the process, have come up with a format for *Gardens to Go* that we like: Show and tell. It may not be original, but it works.

We show you what we have done ourselves and what the six other participating gardeners have done. And with more than a little help from these friends, I explain the rationale behind our decisions. We all agree that learning from other gardeners is the most stimulating and entertaining way to acquire an education. So, welcome to the world of container gardening!

CHAPTER ONE

Pot *by* Pot

Making a Container Garden

In *Bird by Bird*, my favorite book on the subject of writing, author Anne Lamott tells a story that I am going to pass on to you because it also applies to gardening. One Sunday evening when Lamott's brother was ten years old, he sat at the kitchen table close to tears because he had not even begun a school report on birds that was due the next day. Taking pity on the miserable child, their father sat down beside him, put an arm around the boy's shoulders, and said, "Bird by bird, buddy. Just take it bird by bird." That's how to write a book. And it is how to make a container garden. Pot by pot. Most of us start just this way.

By August the tropical plants have enclosed the terrace with walls of foliage and flowers, leaving only a path down the middle.

OPPOSITE: A view of my terrace and garden framed by the overhanging branches of *Brugmansia* 'Charles Grimaldi,' a tender shrub from South America. Brugmansias are container garden favorites, invaluable for their treelike proportions and magnificent trumpet-shaped flowers.

Starting Out

Looking at photographs of our terrace taken in recent years, you might feel overwhelmed and wonder where and how to begin your own garden. There are so many containers, so many unfamiliar plants. But it wasn't always like that. It all started very simply with a few pots of geraniums to add color to a lackluster cement slab twelve feet wide and thirty-three feet long. To relieve the ugliness of the surface and to provide extra seating, we surrounded the slab with a low brick wall.

While the wall improved the looks of the terrace, nothing short of ripping the whole thing up could alter the awkward shape and northern exposure.

As an outdoor living space, the terrace was too narrow for a congenial grouping of garden furniture and too hot for comfort. Due to the position of the summer sun, it bakes for eight hours a day from June to August. While the geraniums loved it, luncheon guests were less enthusiastic. For years we tried umbrellas, and also contemplated an awning, but in the end we gave up and moved all the furniture to the cooling shade of an old apple tree.

Meanwhile, I had recently put a huge kitchen garden back to lawn, so vegetables joined the geraniums on the terrace. I was delighted to have a place to grow beans, tomatoes, squash, cucumbers, and herbs. It was a happy surprise to discover that pretty much anything I had been growing in the ground also prospered in tubs and large pots.

As often happens in gardening, one thing led to another. For some time I had been working on a talk about color in the garden, and containers proved to be the perfect way to try out different combinations of

Taken more than fifteen years ago, this photograph illustrates the first step toward a container garden. A pot of ivy geraniums and a half whiskey barrel of parsley and pansies cheer up an otherwise uninteresting terrace.

Before and after views of the entrance to my container garden.

LEFT: Today the same view shows how partially enclosing the space with a wealth of ornamental plants and adding a cedar arch as an entrance completes the transformation of the terrace into a container garden.

BELOW: Before: barrels provide homes for herbs, cucumbers, snap beans, and other vegetables.

hues. It was easy, instructive, and a great deal of fun. So much so that before long I became hooked. And from a handful of ordinary flowerpots and a few half whiskey barrels, I graduated to an ever-increasing collection of vessels, urns, window boxes, strawberry jars, and containers of every size and description.

I also became much more adventurous in my plant choices. The flames of this new passion were fanned by exposure to a group of young, talented, cutting-edge gardeners, whose excitement about unusual annuals and exotic tropical plants rubbed off on me. And thanks to their generosity with cuttings and seedlings, the plant combinations on the terrace became more and more complex and interesting.

Today

Today the vegetables have disappeared, except for a token patio tomato, and in their place tall cannas shoot up from a ground cover of coleus; elephant's ear, with sooty purple leaves two feet long, rises out of a mass of variegated pink and green sweet potato vine; and the cement surface of the terrace all but vanishes beneath the foliage and flowers of nasturtiums, Mexican flame

The architecture-softening foliage of hyacinth bean, a newcomer to the terrace, cloaks the entrance arch.

OPPOSITE: A clump of Canna 'Tropicanna' (also called 'Phaison') erupts from a molten mass of coleus leaves.

The challenge of empty space, met anew each year, is part of the thrill of container gardening. In May the stage is empty.

By August, plants have given the garden form and structure, filling the void with flowers and foliage.

vine, and other trailing plants. Upright structures, such as the entrance archway and various trellises, groan beneath mantles of morning glories, scarlet runner beans, and other climbers. I audition new vines every year, sometimes with startling consequences.

Once, a vigorous cup-and-saucer vine swamped my husband's espaliered pear tree. The pear grows out of a well in the paved alley between the house and the garage, receiving support from a trellis attached to the garage wall. Delighting in the company of the pear,

the vine sent out eager tendrils that wrapped themselves firmly around the branches of the tree. Soon the pear tree was smothered in dangling purple cups-and-saucers and foliage not of its own making.

For me the thrill of novelty is too alluring to sacrifice room on the terrace for permanent plantings; therefore my container garden remains a summer extravaganza. To a former set designer, there is nothing more exciting than an empty stage, which is why I find

The elements of design that make up a garden should be present even when the plants are grown in pots.

A simple wall of citrus trees in identical pots defines the edge of this garden space.

this kind of garden so fascinating. It is here today, gone tomorrow — a virgin space to be filled anew. There is always something new in the world of horticulture. While this means starting from scratch every year, that's part of the fun. It is astonishing to watch the tropical plants, such as canna, angel's trumpet, and elephant's ear, leap into action. Set out at the end of May or early in June and given regular doses of water-soluble fertilizer, these tender shrubs and perennials, along with fast-growing annuals, shoot up like Jack's beanstalk, becoming well established in a few short weeks.

A large, handsome container surrounded with potted plants rivets the attention of visitors to Pine Meadow Gardens, the Connecticut home and business of garden designer Wesley Rouse.

OPPOSITE: Groups of potted plants, arrayed along the driveway, create a welcoming entrance to Alice Reisenweaver's patio garden.

By the end of July, angel's trumpets have soared to six feet, providing shade with their broad, toothed leaves for the begonias and impatiens at their feet. And in August, when the rest of the garden is looking the worse for wear, the containers are at their lush, floriferous best. Throughout September and well into October, they wax ever more beautiful, until eventually the tenderest of the annuals and warm-climate perennials succumbs to frost. But many prove hardier than expected. Brugmansias, fuchsias, dahlias, and cannas,

along with annuals that enjoy cool temperatures, often hang on until November. Admittedly, it is a sad day when their foliage turns black. But once I've cut it down and transported the roots, rhizomes, and tubers to the cellar for winter storage, my spirits rise. There's always next year.

The season is officially over when the clivia, a couple of unusual geraniums, a very special flowering maple, and the fuchsias, begonias, and various cuttings have made the trip upstairs to a south-facing bedroom, where they will spend the winter under lights. Then, except for a few hardy evergreens in plastic pots and the man-made structures — the archways and trellises, and a small wrought metal table and four chairs — the terrace will remain empty until the new season begins.

Wider Horizons

If this short history of my container garden conveys a fraction of my pleasure in making it, then I am happy. And now that you have glimpsed the possibilities, perhaps you will be willing to go out and buy that first pot. *Gardens to Go* is a joint effort with my partner, Steve Silk, who has become a container garden maker extraordinaire. Together, we propose to show you the way. You will see many photographs of our respective gardens and those of other gardeners. While we want you to enjoy them for what they are, attractive pictures of places and plants, we also think you can learn something from them, as they often illustrate principles of design.

Steve Silk's affinity for the plants and colors of the rain forest is reflected in his multilayered tropical border, which recalls vegetation he admired in South America and Southeast Asia.

If you go along with the definition from *Chambers 20th Century Dictionary* of a garden as "a pleasant spot where flowers are cultivated," you will agree that the only difference between a container garden and one planted in the ground is that the flowers are grown in pots. Otherwise, all the elements of an in-the-ground garden can and should be present: boundaries to define the space, entrances to welcome visitors, accents to focus their attention, and surprises to astonish and delight them.

It is amazing what can be done with an assortment of containers and a small outdoor living space, such as a deck, rooftop, patio, or terrace — the last two terms are used interchangeably throughout the book because they mean the same thing: a paved or surfaced area open to the sky but associated with or part of the domestic architecture.

Of course, Steve and I are only too ready to share our container gardens with you, but we also want you to see what gardeners in very different, and sometimes difficult, situations have accomplished and hear what they have to say. We've tried to find a good balance between gardens on urban rooftops, suburban decks, and country patios. Per Rasmussen gardens on the thirtieth floor of a New Jersey high-rise, Kate Resek on a sliver of Manhattan rooftop wedged in between taller buildings. In suburban Connecticut, Jan Nickel grows all manner of annuals, tender and hardy shrubs, and perennials on a shady deck built by her husband; Lee Anne White does the same on a hot, sunny deck in the outskirts of Atlanta, Georgia, while Mary Stambaugh and Alice Reisenweaver garden near me in semirural settings. Mary's patio overlooks the Connecticut hills; Alice's lies within a stone's throw of the Pootatuck River. When you have seen these wonderful container gardens and have heard from the gardeners themselves, you will want to join in the fun.

To amuse themselves and their visitors, Alex and Joyce Kopper have tucked a lighthearted surprise in among their other containers.

In terms of style, a garden in pots can be anything you want. For instance, Steve wanted a showstopping tropical paradise to remind him of places he had visited as a travel photographer and writer, I wanted an empty stage to fill with a new color scheme every year, Mary wanted a place to entertain friends where she could use the beautiful old pots that came from her grandmother's garden, and Lee Anne White wanted to soften the awkward corners of her expansive Georgia deck and make the space more intimate using grasses and foliage plants.

Besides being extremely personal, container gardens can be of any size or shape; they can cover an entire rooftop or be squeezed onto a tiny patio. They have everything going for them. Assembling them is fun and relatively quick, and anybody can do it. Inexperienced gardeners, daunted by the idea of tackling the out-of-doors, can practice on deck or terrace and gain confidence. Elderly gardeners can enjoy a form of garden making that affords maximum pleasure for minimum physical effort. Even gardeners busy with careers and families can find time for a container garden, and peripatetic gardeners can take their gardens with them.

Whatever your climate, an in-the-ground garden of trees, shrubs, and perennials always means a four-season commitment and year-round work. In temperate zones this involves spring planting, summer maintenance, fall cleanup, and winter protection. A container garden can be tailored to fit the individual gardener's time, energy, and lifestyle. While most of the gardeners in this book concentrate on the summer season and live in the suburbs or the country, city dwellers Per Rasmussen and Kate Resek have risen to the challenge of year-round container gardens. Their experiences and insights will be helpful to other urbanites and to gardeners who want to extend the growing season.

Container gardens are for everyone. Movable, manageable, and versatile, they provide almost instant gratification. Even novices can arrive at a pleasing design with containers simply by moving them around until the arrangement satisfies them. Best of all, mistakes in a container garden can be rectified in minutes instead of backbreaking hours. So if you have been loath to try your hand at garden making for lack of experience or some other foolish reason, hesitate no longer.

PRECEDING PAGE: Mary Stambaugh sees her container garden as a place to entertain friends and an opportunity to use a collection of heirloom flowerpots.

ABOVE: Clustered in corners and around columns, grasses and foliage plants serve to reduce the size of Lee Anne White's Georgia deck and make the space more intimate and appealing.

OPPOSITE: For me the challenge is to limit the hues but expand the range of plants to create a different "set" every season.

the Art *of the* Possible

Regulations, Access, Water Source, Drainage, and Exposure

Before we get started, a word to the wise. Although there are precious few places where a container garden is out of the question, they do exist. Sadly, friends of ours who own a condo in New York City were denied permission to put planters on their balcony by the board of their building. But another friend, who lives in Maryland and designs container gardens for clients in the Baltimore area, has never encountered such a restriction. So a lot depends on the specific circumstances and where you live. When problems do occur, they usually involve weight or water. Large containers full of earth are heavy and could exceed the load-bearing capacity

Hedged in by neighboring buildings, Kate Resek's green oasis provides cooling summer shade and year-round peace, keeping New York City at bay with vine-clad walls and broadleaf evergreens.

of some balconies and even rooftops. As for water, according to Linda Yang, author of *The City Gardener's Handbook*, the bible for urban gardeners, "Water seepage has plagued the upstairs gardener since the Hanging Gardens of Babylon." Nevertheless, if you take a helicopter ride around Manhattan, you will discover a whole green world up there — so do not despair.

Regulations

The sensible thing to do, if you live in the city and want to make a container garden above street level, is to go through the proper channels. Designer Marilyn Rennagel, a friend and weekend neighbor, describes the steps she took before installing a rooftop garden for a client in lower Manhattan. "First I talked to the

Lee Anne White's elevated deck was pronounced sound and awaits its complement of furniture and potted plants and the installation of a water garden made from a drinking trough for cattle.

OPPOSITE: Thirty stories above the ground on Per Rasmussen's terrace, more than two hundred potted plants, none the worse for their journey up in the elevator, bask in the summer sun.

building management company about adding weight to the structure. I had designed modular decking, with an eighth of an inch between the boards to allow water to go through to the asphalt roof, which had excellent drainage."

After the initial meeting, the company consulted their civil engineer, who okayed the project — the roof had always been intended as usable living space. Marilyn then submitted working drawings to the company, which gave her their blessing. A tenant in the building who wanted to garden in pots would find it all much simpler and quicker than a hired professional proposing new construction. However, to avoid a potentially expensive, embarrassing mistake, it is always better to talk to the building management company before investing in containers, plants, and potting soil.

"Once you have permission," says Marilyn, "alert the building superintendent. In fact, make him your new best friend. You are going to be bringing a whole lot of stuff through his lobby to the elevator, and you want him on your side." She also suggests laying paper across the lobby to keep the floor clean and acquiring a little red wagon to transport your supplies.

City rooftops and balconies present the most problems for the container gardener, but Lee Anne White says that even a deck can raise safety issues. Her deck has to support substantial wooden furniture, about a hundred large potted plants, and an extremely heavy water feature, made from a drinking trough for cattle. "When we bought our house," she says, "it had just been inspected. But it is a good idea to check with a local building inspector before loading up an elevated deck."

Site Analysis

With weight and water problems out of the way, you are ready for the next step, site analysis. In the best of all possible worlds, your patio, deck, or rooftop would be easy to get to from the outside world; it would boast a convenient source of running water; and the flooring would be properly laid, impervious to moisture, and pitched so that excess water would drain safely away from the walls of your house or apartment building. Real life being what it is, most patios, decks, and rooftops leave something to be desired as container garden sites.

Nevertheless, the gardeners in this book have found ways of pushing, hauling, wheeling, rolling, or dragging whatever they need up and down hills and stairs, into elevators, and through apartment house lobbies.

They have used their ingenuity to bring water to their gardens and have taken corrective measures to improve poor drainage. Their enthusiasm and good cheer will encourage you, while their experiences will give you ideas for coping with your own less-than-perfect site.

Access

Once again, urbanites who garden above the first floor have the most to overcome. There is no elevator in Kate Resek's building. To reach her container garden, you have to climb a steep, narrow flight of stairs, proceed through her living room and kitchen, and exit out the back door onto the roof. Hauling plants and potting soil up the stairs is not easy, but since she spends her summers in the city, it is worth it. In that noisy, lively, colorful but harsh environment, her garden provides a leafy place of rest and relaxation.

Even where there is an elevator, access through an apartment building can mean innumerable journeys across the lobby with your little red wagon. And don't forget, what goes up must come down. Spent annuals, clippings, and other debris must make the journey down to the basement garbage room. Per Rasmussen, who lives on the thirtieth floor of his building, uses a hand truck and makes literally hundreds of trips a season, up and down, through the rooms in his own apartment, into the elevator, and across the lobby.

Large apartment buildings often have freight elevators, which are a boon to container gardeners, but according to Marilyn Rennagel, they are always in demand.

Lee Anne White finds negotiating the four steps to her deck hard work when she is loaded down with heavy pots. But her container garden is worth the effort for the charm and intimacy it brings to an otherwise spare, empty space.

OPPOSITE: Mary Stambaugh's patio is easy to reach from her driveway and greenhouse despite being two steps above grade.

A level site makes container gardening easier. Steve Silk was able to create a potting area handy to the driveway and just around the corner from his patio.

"Not a day goes by that work isn't being done in these buildings, and the super has to balance the needs of a gardener against the needs of all those workmen. So you have to make an appointment to use the freight elevator."

In addition, every building has its own little anomalies. In one, where Marilyn was installing six-foot trees on a penthouse terrace, she discovered that the elevator only went up as far as the thirtieth floor. Unfortunately, the terrace was on the thirty-first. She and her partner had to push and pull the trees the rest of the way up a flight of stairs on a hand truck. "And we did it! The two of us." This can-do attitude helps if you are a city gardener. But you don't have to live on the top floor to find stairs a curse.

Although there are only four steps leading to Lee Anne White's deck, she finds lugging materials up and down them more than enough work. "A wheelbarrow gets the pots, plants, and supplies to the bottom of the steps. From there, most can be lifted onto the deck, where I can use a dolly to wheel things around. My biggest challenge is handling the tender plants. They are a pain to move at the end of one season and the beginning of the next because, left in their pots, they are extremely heavy. My husband helps me make the transition from ground level to deck and vice versa. But I'm leaning more and more toward permanent plantings."

Steps always create problems for the container gardener. I know, because our terrace is built into a slope. One end is shored by a four-foot retaining wall with steps down to the lawn. The steps are the shortest route to the cellar, where I store pots and plants for the winter. The other end of the terrace affords level access to and from the driveway, but everything that arrives by car or truck has to be maneuvered through the enclosed breezeway without letting out a determined Jack Russell terrier.

Steve has a better-behaved dog and a more convenient arrangement. His level site makes it an easy trip from the driveway to an enviable backstage potting area and cold frame, which are just around the corner from the patio. "When I order sand and compost by the truckload, I'll bring the wheelbarrow to the driveway," he says, "and mix everything on the spot, then wheel it straight to the patio. Or I'll mix it up in the potting area, where I can make as much mess as I want, plant the containers there, then carry them around onto the patio."

Mary Stambaugh's hilltop site is gently terraced. A few steps down from the house, the patio rests on a flat semicircular platform of earth supported by a low retaining wall. At one end, there are two shallow steps; the other end is flush with the ground. While the patio

is readily accessible from the driveway and greenhouse, it is a long way from her compost bins. And Mary, like Steve, concocts her own potting soil from compost and sand. These ingredients have to be transported by wheelbarrow the long way around to take advantage of the level end of the patio.

Water Source

Water is the lifeblood of a container garden. Therefore, nothing is more important than a convenient source, like an outdoor faucet right on the terrace. But this is not always possible. For Kate Resek, watering her pots is a real labor of love. She has to attach a hose to the kitchen faucet, thread it through the open window, and drag it around the terrace to her plants. Fortunately, her garden is so shady that she can usually get away with watering every second or third day.

Mary Stambaugh and I are fortunate enough to have spigots on our respective terraces, but we still do a good deal of hose lugging. Indeed, hoses are the bane of every container gardener's existence. They kink, coil and uncoil, knock over pots, and generally wreak havoc in small, crowded spaces. But unless you install a drip irrigation system, as Lee Anne White and Steve have done, hoses are here to stay. Last year I experimented with a polyurethane hose that coils itself up automatically. It was a tidy-looking affair that stretched to fifty feet, but the half-inch-diameter tubing delivered water so slowly that it would have taken all day to do the pots. So I returned it.

Drip irrigation is the way to go, if you have enough water pressure and enough patience (see chapter 8). But you still need a nearby water source. Steve had the foresight to run a line to his potting area and, at the same time, to put in an outdoor shower. Even if he does

Handsome new pavers, properly laid and correctly pitched, solved the drainage problems on Per Rasmussen's rooftop terrace.

have to resort to the hose occasionally, it isn't too arduous. "If I get hot dragging the hose around," he says smugly, "I just hop in the shower."

Drainage

Container gardeners have a love/hate relationship with water. While it is the lifeblood of a potted garden, in the wrong place it can cause damage and result in

expensive repairs. Per Rasmussen spent a small fortune resurfacing his rooftop. "Originally it had twelve inches of concrete and a waterproof barrier under pavers, which were cemented together so they had a nice finished look. But there was only one drain, and by the time my partner and I bought the apartment, the terrace was in a bad state of repair." Eventually the whole thing had to be redone to correct the pitch and provide adequate drainage.

Rooftop gardens are the most prone to water problems, but they can also occur at ground level, as Steve discovered with his flagstone patio. He and his wife, Kate, with the help of a stalwart friend, laid the huge, irregular Bucks County flagstones themselves. To the naked eye the site looked perfectly level, but it proved otherwise. "When the builders graded around the house," says Steve, "they filled in next to the foundation but couldn't get the machinery close enough to

Mary Stambaugh is spared drainage problems because rainwater and water from the containers seep harmlessly through the gravel and into the ground.

pack down the earth. So that part of the terrace has settled two or three inches. It should slope gradually away from the house — and most of it does, but the part nearest the foundation is too low." To prevent water from finding its way into the house, he installed a perforated pipe in the two-foot-wide swath of gravel between the foundation and the terrace and, for good measure, laid drain pipes in the gravel under the stone patio.

Mary Stambaugh is one of the happy few with no drainage problems. To make the patio, she simply had the turf removed and two different grades of pea gravel, one coarse and one fine, spread four inches deep. She edged the semicircle with large flat rocks, and that was all there was to it. The two grades mingled to form a stable mixture that stays in place. The surface is firm and pleasant to walk on; maintenance is minimal; and water drains quickly and harmlessly into the earth beneath the gravel.

Our poured-concrete terrace may be short on charm, but it is long on maintenance-free durability and good drainage. A slight tilt away from the house and numerous openings at the base of the brick wall allow excess water to run off onto the lawn. The surface is easy to clean: it can be swept or hosed off in a few minutes, and you never have to worry about saucers under your potted plants.

Wood is less forgiving. "I learned that the hard way," says a rueful Lee Anne White. "One of the quickest ways to ruin your flooring is to place pots directly on the wood surface without protection. Containers should either be raised on pot feet or bricks or placed in saucers. Otherwise, water soaks through the bottom of the pot straight into the wood. This both stains the wood and encourages rot." She adds that periodically decks should be treated with a sealer, whether you have containers on them or not.

Sun, Shade, and Exposure

I hope you haven't been frightened off by the talk of safety issues and water problems, because now you are home free. You only need one more piece of information before taking yourself and your credit card off to the nearest nursery or garden center: in order to buy the right plants, you need to know whether your site is sunny or shady. Whichever it is, there are plants suited to those conditions. All you have to do is match the plant to the site, which you can do by reading the nursery labels. The light requirements of each plant are given as either *full sun*, *full shade*, or *part shade*.

Of course, one of the perks of container gardening is flexibility. If you have inadvertently put a shade-loving

SUN AND SHADE DEFINED

Per Rasmussen's south-facing terrace, which lies open to the heavens (and is halfway there), is the very definition of *full sun*. In other words, there is sun all day long. The vast majority of annuals that we grow for their flowers, and most flowering perennials, both tender and hardy, like full sun. However, they will do almost as well in as little as five hours of sun during the hottest, brightest part of the day — from midmorning to midafternoon. And most sun lovers are reasonably content with either sun all morning or sun all afternoon.

Shade is a bit more complicated, as there are varying degrees of shade. Surrounded by tall buildings on all sides, Kate Resek's garden almost meets the criteria for *full shade*, but not quite. *Full shade* means a substantial reduction in light for the entire day. But in the city, reflected light from the walls and windows of surrounding buildings brightens even the darkest situation. *Part shade* doesn't tell the gardener much. You have to know which part is which. Many shade-loving plants can tolerate morning sun and an east-facing situation. But the same plants would burn to a crisp in a western exposure because afternoon sun is much hotter than morning sun. Therefore, exposed rooftop gardens and west-facing sites are never suitable for plants that need or prefer shade, unless protection can be provided by trees or an overhead structure like Per's gazebo.

plant in too much sun, you can move it. All you have to do is find that one sheltered corner, protected by a bit of overhanging roof, and set your gasping impatiens in its kindly shadow. Or if you are in Kate's situation, you have to make the most of every sunbeam. "I used to get some sunlight," she says, "until the restaurant down below had to put up a vent as tall as the building. Now, during the summer, I only get about an hour and a half a day of direct sun." But in the brightest spot, a crab apple blooms generously in May, followed by mountain laurels in June.

While a container garden can be manipulated to take advantage of difficult light conditions, it is easier to go with the flow, which is why Kate sticks to plants with a strong preference for shade and Per chooses sun lovers.

Wind

Wind is the enemy on Per's terrace. His trees blew over so often that he had to chain them to the parapet. And he gave up on terra-cotta containers because so many got broken. At ground level, wind is much less troublesome. But north-easters and early tropical storms have often top-pled the brugmansias on my terrace. To save his banana trees from a similar fate, Steve uses a heavy potting mix and puts rocks in the bottom of the pots, a trick that should work for you if your site is relatively protected. However, in an exposed situation like Per's, you might consider tethering your tall plants and erecting some sort of windbreak, such as sections of fencing or lattice panels.

OPPOSITE: Shade-loving astilbe, ferns, pachysandra, impatiens, and woodbine are happy on Kate Resek's rooftop, which receives almost no direct sun.

Geraniums, which belong to the genus *Pelargonium* and are among the most colorful of all bedding plants, bloom luxuri-antly on Per Rasmussen's sun-drenched terrace.

CHAPTER THREE

Mainstays

Basic Plants for the Container Garden

Ready, set, go! Straight to the garden center. But first — not all plants are created equal. Some that look utterly beguiling as babies snuggled in their four-inch pots become messy, tedious container specimens that need constant attention. If you succumb to frilly, large-flowered petunias or to impatiens that look like adorable little rosebuds, prepare to clean up after them all summer long. But go ahead anyway. Finding out how plants behave is easy in containers and part of the fun.

Nevertheless, to make a real garden, you will need a repertoire of plants that maintain their good looks *without* constant grooming, that exude health

More glamorous than familiar dracaena, New Zealand flax, with its colorful swords of foliage, performs the starring role in this container planting.

OPPOSITE: Hollandia Nursery in Connecticut caters to container gardeners, offering them an enormous array of tempting possibilities.

and vigor and are capable of sustained performance. These are your mainstays. Their job, if they are flowering plants, is to bloom long and generously. If they are foliage plants, their leaves or needles must remain in pristine condition throughout the growing season, and if they are evergreens, beyond.

Seasonal Gardens

Which plants will become mainstays in your container garden depends on the kind of garden you have in mind. Here are three possibilities. You can do what Steve and I do. Essentially, our container gardening season lasts from June until November because we use annuals and tender perennials. These plants give us an opportunity to go overboard, try out new color schemes, experiment with unfamiliar plants, and make our ordinary surroundings look exotic, exuberant, and different every year. If a color scheme proves a disaster or some new plant turns out to be a dog, it doesn't matter. With annuals and tender perennials, you are never stuck with your mistakes. You can always bid them adieu in the fall and start all over in the spring with a new palette of plants and a different garden theme. For us, that's the whole point. But Steve lives in the suburbs, I live in a semirural setting, and we both have other gardens.

Kate Resek has only her rooftop; therefore her priorities are different. She wants a container garden that gives her something to look at all year. Nor does she favor change for its own sake. "I have enough structure

Steve Silk's summer extravaganza features plants from tropical and subtropical America, Africa, Asia, and Australia, bringing an exotic flavor to his Connecticut containers.

OPPOSITE: This Alberta spruce, one of a pair, spent three contented years in its pot, waiting for a permanent home in the landscape.

now, so that I don't have to start from scratch every season," she says. "The trees, mountain laurels, and rhododendrons are here to stay, but I do experiment with different annuals and rearrange the smaller pots every summer."

Per Rasmussen is in a similar position. The terrace is his only garden, and he doesn't want it to be bare for six months of the year. So he has established a year-round framework of evergreen shrubs and trees, which also serves as a backdrop for summer flowers. While he always plants geraniums and tries a few new annuals every year, the main display is provided by hardy perennials, which he divides and replants as needed, giving away extra divisions to friends.

Different gardeners. Different approaches. But no matter what type of garden you choose, you will need a palette of basic plants. For the benefit of four-season container gardeners, we have included in this chapter hardy plants, both herbaceous and woody, that can withstand the rigors of winter in pots and planters.

The plants are divided into four categories: dwarf conifers and broadleaf evergreens, small deciduous trees, ornamental grasses and other hardy perennials, annuals and tender perennials. But don't let these categories inhibit you. Feel free to mix, match, and experiment with annuals, hardy and tender perennials, and woody plants in your container garden.

There are often a few shrubs and hardy herbaceous plants among the annuals and tender perennials on my terrace. A pair of small Alberta spruces spent three years in pots, one on either side of the main entrance, where they were perfectly happy until they found their place in the landscape. And for several years, hostas and ornamental grasses were fixtures of the container garden. They contributed their varied textures and foliage colors to the summer scene while I waited for a decline in the vole population before returning them to the ground.

Overview of Per Rasmussen's terrace garden, where dwarf conifers fulfill their roles as both accents and background plants.

OPPOSITE: To lead the way up to her greenhouse door, Mary Stambaugh selected arborvitae 'Smaragd' ('Emerald Green'), a narrow, upright cultivar that will remain slender and shapely and even tolerate pruning if necessary.

Dwarf Conifers and Broadleaf Evergreens

Dwarf conifers are the backbone of Per's sunny exposed container garden, where you will see them playing a variety of roles, depending on their shapes and forms. Beneath an elegant structure of steel tubing, a solid cone of Alberta spruce (*Picea glauca* 'Conica') serves as a focal point, its dark bulk drawing attention to the contrasting grace and lightness of the archway above.

Hardy to Zone 4, dwarf spruces come in many forms and different tones of blue and green: *P. pungens* 'Fat Albert' has a perfect conical shape and blue needles; *P. glauca* 'Little Globe' forms a neat ball and has short, dense light green needles; *P. pungens* 'Iseli Fastigate,' with blue needles, grows into a very narrow and upright column reaching a height of about twelve feet in ten to fifteen years. It receives high marks as an accent plant. Slow growing by nature, these and other spruces of reduced size are undemanding and seem indifferent to becoming pot-bound, as long as they are fed once a year and watered as necessary.

In another part of the Rasmussen garden, a hedge of upright juniper (*Juniperus*) creates a uniform blue-green background for a small fountain and vivid pink geraniums. Sun-loving junipers are cold tolerant to Zone 3 and come in different colors and forms. *Juniperus communis* 'Pencil Point,' which has silver-blue needles and grows to a slender six feet, has a bright yellow cousin, *J. communis* 'Gold Cone,' also narrow and upright. Both are attention getters and can be used as exclamation marks in a container garden.

While upright junipers are useful as screening as well as accents, trailing forms bring the container garden down to earth. For this purpose, try one of the following: *J. horizontalis* 'Wiltonii,' also called 'blue rug juniper'; golden 'Mother Lode'; or my favorite, ground-hugging *J. procumbens* 'Nana,' with short, crowded sea green needles.

Mary Stambaugh wanted her front patio to be attractive and welcoming all year and chose slender, shapely arborvitae (*Thuja occidentalis*) for the job. These tough, tolerant evergreens are hardy from Zones 3 to 7 and have proved to be excellent trees for difficult situations. In *The City Gardener's Handbook*, Linda Yang offers this evidence of their fortitude: "The arborvitae on a neighbor's penthouse terrace survived both burning sun and vicious winds. Reputed to prefer moist soil, this one never noticed when its owner forgot to water."

Cultivars of arborvitae come in green and gold and assume many shapes, from narrow pyramids, like slow-growing *T. occidentalis* 'Degroot's Spire' and 'Smaragd' (also called 'Emerald Green'), to round balls, like 'Little Gem' and 'Little Giant.' 'Reingold' is a conical

form with golden foliage, and 'Yellow Ribbon' is a narrow cone shape with foliage tipped in bright yellow.

Two sun-loving pines also made it into Steve's and my "basics" list. Per appreciates the endurance of easy, adaptable mugos (*Pinus mugo*), which survived wind, heat, and all manner of rough handling by the workmen who replaced his roof a few years ago. Marilyn Rennagel waxes eloquent on behalf of the extremely slow-growing bristlecone pine, *Pinus aristata*, which she describes as a "wonderful tree, with an interesting, irregular form and dark needles, that should be used more often." *P. aristata* grows well from Zone 4 to Zone 7, and the mugos can take it one zone colder. According to Michael Dirr in his superb *Manual of Woody Landscape Plants*, the bristlecone pine, a native of our sunny Southwest, actively dislikes shade, thus it would not do on Kate Resek's terrace.

Kate's picks are all shade-tolerant broadleaf evergreens that are hardy in Zones 5 and 6: rhododendrons, azaleas, native mountain laurels, and Japanese andromedas. Rhododendrons are nearest and dearest to her heart. "I had just bought my first one when my neighbor

Pale pink flower clusters adorn this dwarf rhododendron, a Yaku hybrid, resulting from a cross between low-growing species from Japan and China.

OPPOSITE: Rhododendrons provide an evergreen background for colorful foliage plants on Kate Resek's rooftop.

offered me another. It had been living on her fire escape in violation of the codes, so she asked me if I would give it a home. I said, 'Absolutely!' And that's how it all began."

The genus *Rhododendron*, which includes azaleas, is enormous, with as many as eight hundred species. Therefore it is not surprising that there is a huge variety in size and plant habit. Some are large-leaved and are the size of trees, while others barely come up to an adult's knee and have leaves the size of a baby's fingernails. Hybrids derived from *Rhododendron yakushimanum*, a dwarf species from the Japanese island of Yakushima, are particularly well suited to container gardens. The so-called Yaku hybrids remain small in stature and have superb foliage — dark green and glossy above, lined with soft, fawn-colored indumentum (feltlike hairs) underneath. The flowers come in white and different shades of pink. 'Yaku Princess' has apple blossom pink flowers turning white; 'Yaku Prince' and 'Yaku King' both have pink flowers.

Evergreen azaleas, ranging in height from eighteen inches to three feet, also make good container subjects. Low growing, densely twiggy, and well furnished with small, shiny leaves, they offer year-round good looks and lovely pink, red, or white flowers early in the season: 'Gumpo Pink' has a low, domelike profile; 'Hino-Crimson' is an old favorite with a mounding habit; 'Sir Robert' becomes a compact three-by-three-foot plant bearing large pink flowers.

In the wild, mountain laurels tend to be leggy plants, but giant strides have been made in the introduction of plants that are fuller and shapelier. Geneticist and plant breeder Richard Jaynes has created dozens of delightful new garden forms of this magnificent native plant. Of particular interest to container gardeners are the miniatures he has developed from *Kalmia latifolia*. All are hardy to Zone 5.

'Little Linda' has shiny, dark green leaves only an inch and a half long on a bushy two-foot plant with a spread of about three feet. The flowers are deep cerise pink in bud and open to a paler pink; 'Minuet' boasts a circular pattern of cinnamon red within each open, cup-shaped flower on a plant similar in habit to 'Little Linda.' Other miniatures include 'Elf,' with white flowers, pink-flowered 'Tinkerbell,' and 'Tiddlywinks.'

Like the rhododendrons, azaleas, and mountain laurels, andromedas (*Pieris japonica*) belong to the heath family and have shiny evergreen leaves. But instead of dome-shaped flower trusses (clusters) resting on platforms of leaves, the tiny semiclosed bells hang in gracefully drooping panicles from the tips of the stems. The color of the flowers is either white or pale pink, and there are many cultivars. Hardy to Zones 5 and 6, andromedas dislike wind and would therefore be a poor choice in an exposed situation, such as on Per's rooftop.

Kate Resek has enclosed one end of her city garden with small deciduous trees and shrubs, like the serviceberry (right), which provides overhead privacy, and an oakleaf hydrangea (left), which partially conceals the surrounding lattice wall.

OPPOSITE: Evergreen azalea 'Delaware Valley White' flowers on the steps to Mary Stambaugh's front door, with extra-hardy boxwood (*Buxus microphylla* 'Tide Hill') in the foreground.

Small Deciduous Trees

Dwarf Japanese maples (*Acer palmatum dissectum*) are the crème de la crème of small trees for container gardens with their beautiful zigzag branching pattern and elegant, lacy foliage that turns gorgeous colors in the fall. However, they must have afternoon shade, shelter from the wind, and winter protection. 'Crimson Queen' eventually becomes a five-foot spreading mound of finely cut dark red foliage that blazes crimson in October; 'Viridis' has a similar habit, lacy green

Dwarf cut-leaf Japanese maples are among the most elegant of small trees for sheltered, shady patios. Beautiful in all seasons, they offer an interesting winter silhouette, lacy summer foliage, and vivid fall coloring.

RIGHT: The scented flowers of witch hazel (*Hamamelis* x *intermedia* 'Arnold Promise') open as early as February in Zone 6.

OPPOSITE: Hardy blue oat grass is just as much at home in a pot on my terrace as it is in the perennial border.

leaves, and orange autumn coloring. Both are hardy to the warmer sections of Zone 5.

Serviceberry, or shadbush (*Amelanchier canadensis*), can be considered either a small multistemmed tree or a tall shrub, which is cold tolerant to Zone 3. It is easy to grow and has smooth, slender gray stems; small, slightly blue-green leaves; and, fleetingly, little clusters of white flowers in the spring. Its value for the container gardener is its undemanding nature and the dappled shade it casts, along with its attractive yellow-orange fall color.

Witch hazels (*Hamamelis*) have it all. Hardy at least as far north as Boston, these relatively small, vase-shaped trees offer early spring flowers and fall color. My favorite is the Chinese witch hazel (*Hamamelis mollis*), which can bloom as early as February in Connecticut, displaying knots of scented, yellow, threadlike flowers. The fall leaf color is a pure, deep gold. Many cultivars have been developed from crosses between the Chinese and Japanese witch hazel. Of these, yellow-flowered *H.* x *intermedia*

'Arnold Promise' is the most familiar; 'Diane' has dark bronze-red flowers; and 'Jelena,' which also rejoices in the name 'Copper Beauty,' has golden orange flowers.

Linda Yang is a fan of the crab apples (*Malus* spp.), which she claims in *The City Gardener's Handbook* "cheerfully survive unspeakable neglect on rooftops and yards." Indeed, a crab apple was one of the plants she recommended for Kate Resek's garden. As there are innumerable cultivars, look for those described as resistant to rust, mildew, and fire blight. *Malus sargentii*, an old variety, is still one of the most disease resistant and has a naturally dwarf habit. The abundant spring flowers are white. 'Red Jade' is a beautiful weeping form with good disease resistance, pink to white flowers, and a fine display of red fruit in the fall. 'Louisa' has pink flowers, a somewhat weeping habit, and good disease resistance. All are suitable for Zones 4 to 7.

Ornamental Grasses and Other Hardy Perennials

In her wonderful book *Ornamental Grasses: The Amber Wave*, Carole Ottesen says that all ornamental grasses make good container subjects. Certainly Lee Anne White is enthusiastic about them for her hot, sunny Georgia deck, and *Miscanthus sinensis* 'Morning Light' tops the list. "Not only is it beautiful and hardy," says Lee Anne, "but it is a little smaller than many other miscanthus species, making it more suitable for a deck-sized space. Mine seems very content in its pot."

Grasses are high on Per's list, too. Feather reed grass (*Calamagrostis* x *acutiflora* 'Stricta') is a favorite for its narrow, upright form and slender flower spikes in June. Green and white striped ribbon grass (*Phalaris arundinacea* 'Picta'), which can be an aggressive men-

ace in a perennial border, behaves beautifully and looks smashing confined to its white wooden planters (see pages 34–35). Blue oat grass (*Helictotrichon semper-virens*) is welcome anywhere with its narrow, upright powder blue blades and has been a winner in my container garden. Shade-tolerant Japanese forest grass (*Hakonechloa macra* 'Aureola'), which becomes a low, arching mound of yellow and green striped foliage, grows as well in pots as in the ground.

Perennial fountain grass (*Pennisetum alopecuroides*) is a natural for pot culture, forming a handsome, symmetrical mound of fine foliage. It blooms late in the

OPPOSITE: *Pennisetum setaceum* 'Rubrum' adds its fine dark red foliage and fuzzy, arching flower heads to Steve Silk's tropical border.

Miscanthus sinensis 'Morning Light' (background right) contributes an elegant fountain of slender blades to the water-garden setting on Lee Anne White's Georgia deck.

Against an evergreen background, perennial coreopsis and rudbeckia combined with annuals and tender sweet potato vine enjoy the sun on Per Rasmussen's rooftop.

OPPOSITE: Hostas, liriope, and ferns thrive in pots in a shady corner of Alex and Joyce Koppers' garden.

season with a sunburst of fuzzy tails on slightly arching stems. Its annual relation, *P. setaceum* 'Rubrum,' which has dark red blades and red flower heads, is already popular with container gardeners.

Lee Anne finds handsome but invasive bamboos perfect container subjects. "When I grow them in pots," she says, "I *know* that they're under control. I have two short varieties plus the fishpole or golden bamboo (*Phyllostachys aurea*), which is about fifteen feet tall. The pygmy bamboo (*Pleioblastus pygmaeus*) is only sixteen inches high, with a spread of three feet. And *P. auricoma*, another dwarf, is about the same height, with green and yellow variegated leaves. All three have overwintered beautifully here in Zone 7."

A rundown of highly satisfactory perennials blooming in Per's summer garden will give you more ideas for your container garden: sea pink (*Armeria caespitosa*); daylilies (*Hemerocallis cultivars*); bulbous lilies (*Lilium* ssp.), especially the so-called midcentury hybrids, such as orange 'Enchantment,' golden yellow 'Croesus,' and red 'Cinnabar'; black-eyed Susans (*Rudbeckia fulgida sullivantii* 'Goldsturm'); coreopsis cultivars, including *Coreopsis verticillata* 'Moonbeam' and 'Zagreb'; boltonia (*Boltonia asteroides* 'Snowbank'); false dragonhead (*Physostegia virginiana*); and a slew of herbs, including tansy (*Tanacetum*), English lavender (*Lavandula angustifolia*), chives (*Allium schoenoprasum*), thyme (*Thymus vulgaris*), sage (*Salvia officinalis*), and parsley (*Petroselinum crispum*).

Although Per has no shade, except under the gazebo, he wouldn't be without hostas. "Their leaves are wonderful," he says, "but I cut off all the flowering stalks because the spent blossoms stick to the foliage and make such a mess on the terrace." Other shade-tolerant perennials that take kindly to containers include grassy lilyturf (*Liriope muscari*) with either dark

green or variegated cream and green leaves; alumroot (*Heuchera* spp.), with dozens of cultivars, such as 'Green Spice' and 'Pewter Veil'; hardy ferns; and, of course, ivies, of which there are many with attractive variegated leaves.

Annuals and Tender Perennials

Now we come to Steve's and my bailiwick, annuals and tender perennials, the colorful superstars. Steve's description of the dramatic red Abyssinian banana (*Ensete ventricosum* 'Maurelii') makes it all but irresistible as the centerpiece in a container garden: "Bananas of all stripes are fun, but this one is by far the best, with the thickest foliage, which holds up to wind, and deep wine red coloration that is superlative when backlit. It easily grows to ten or twelve feet, with leaves four feet long and maybe eighteen inches wide." Now, there's a plant that makes a statement!

Cannas are a mutual favorite for their statuesque proportions and large, dramatic leaves, which can be as colorful as their flowers. Red-flowered 'Australia' has solid-colored foliage of the deepest, darkest red imaginable, while 'Tropicanna' ('Phaison'), which has orange flowers, combines bonfire hues in its striped leaves. Fittingly, 'Bengal Tiger' also has striped leaves, yellow and green in this case, edged with a fine red line. The flowers are orange. And 'Pink Sunburst,' with salmon-pink flowers and foliage similar to 'Bengal Tiger,' includes pink shades among the yellow and green stripes. To this brief list, Steve adds 'Intrigue,' which can reach eight feet in height and has "long, lance-shaped leaves of a nice deep burgundy." By virtue of their stature, substance, and sculptural quality, cannas earn their place in a container garden as back-

TOP: The sculptural leaves of *Canna* 'Bengal Tiger' (also called 'Pretoria') boast a fine red edging.

BOTTOM: Canna 'Tropicanna,' paired with matching blood-flower (*Asclepias curassavica*), a milkweed relation from South America, creates a symphony in red and orange.

OPPOSITE: Red Abyssinian banana on Steve Silk's patio, with a ground cover of sweet potato vine and 'Lemon Gem' marigolds.

Large, shaggy cactus-type dahlias are featured players in Steve Silk's tropical border.

RIGHT: 'Bishop of Llandaff' (upper right), a small-flowered single red dahlia, performs with an ensemble cast of mainstays: coleus (center foreground), variegated parlor maple (lower right), elephant's ear (upper left), canna (center), and brugmansia (top center).

drops and corner keepers or in flanking positions at entry points.

Steve and I are both devotees of dahlias, which, as he puts it, "offer plenty of floral firepower and come in every color but blue, with a host of varied forms." These run the gamut from little round balls of petals to giant, spiky cactus types. Other desirable family traits include variety in terms of height, from lofty six-footers to dwarf "patio" plants, and superb dark green, bronze, or dark red foliage. Steve likes the shaggy double flower forms, and we both are fond of small, single 'Bishop of Llandaff,' an old-fashioned cultivar with red flowers and dark red leaves.

Parlor maples (*Abutilon* spp.), which have been beloved as houseplants for more than a century, also

Tower Hill Botanic Garden in Massachusetts provides inspiration for container gardeners with its unusual plant choices and imaginative combinations.

LEFT: A shower of apricot bells and bright variegated foliage makes *Abutilon pictum* 'Thompsonii' the perfect choice with minipetunia look-alikes (*Callibracoa*) in the same color family and yellow-green sweet potato vine.

The semitrailing *A. megapotamicum* 'Variegatum' drapes itself over a corner of this wooden container (lower left).

make wonderful outdoor container subjects. The bushy, shrublike plants are covered all season with flush after flush of tissue-paper bells in a lovely range of colors: pink, red, yellow, peach, orange, and white. The sharply lobed leaves are convincingly maplelike and come in solid green and mottled yellow and green (see photo above). Plant heights and habits vary. Low-growing 'Bartley Schwartz,' with peach-pink flowers, cascades gracefully from a pot or hanging basket; *A. pictum* 'Thompsonii' is upright in carriage and has soft orange flowers and variegated yellow and green leaves; and semitrailing *A. megapotamicum* 'Variegatum,' also with mottled green and yellow foliage, offers a change of pace in flower form. The small, dangling, fuchsia-like

blossoms have puffy bright red calyxes from which short, pale yellow skirts emerge.

Fuchsia is another conservatory favorite that flourishes outdoors in containers, producing innumerable bell-within-a-bell flowers from early summer to late fall. A magnet to humming birds, *Fuchsia triphylla* 'Gartenmeister Bonstedt' has narrow, tubular red flowers in which the skirt of petals barely peeks out from beneath the four sepals. And there are the countless fuchsia cultivars, with large blossoms and extravagantly frilled skirts emerging from beneath the sepals. The plant habit of the genus varies from trailing to upright. Many lend themselves to pruning and are easy to make into standards.

Lantana (*Lantana camara*) is another shrubby plant ideally suited to container culture. The blossoms consist of minute five-lobed flowers arranged in tight, flat clusters. They come in combinations of red and orange or yellow and pink and in solid yellow, orange, and mauve. The rough, leathery leaves can be dark green or variegated, like *L. montevidensis* 'Samantha,' which has yellow and green foliage and matching yellow flowers. Popular for hanging baskets, lantanas are also useful for draping over the edges of pots and threading among other plants. Like fuchsias, they can even be trained as standards.

Upright, spirelike plants for container gardens are always in short supply, which is why *Angelonia angustifolia* is such a find. How did I ever live without this plant? It has not yet acquired a common name but is sure to become well known for its fabulously long season of bloom. The individual flowers will fascinate anyone who takes the time to gaze into their little flat, orchidlike faces. The branched spires reach a height of

Lantanas are popular for hanging baskets and in mixed containers. Many cultivars come in this fiery combination of red and orange.

LEFT: 'Samantha' spreads a bright skirt of yellow blossoms and variegated leaves at the feet of taller plants on Steve Silk's patio.

OPPOSITE: An urn, designed for a client by Wesley Rouse of Pine Meadow Gardens in Connecticut, overflows with *Fuchsia* 'Gartenmeister Bonstedt,' ivy geranium, and variegated potato vine (*Solanum jasminoides* 'Variegata').

two feet and can either stand on their own or mingle gracefully with other plants. The flower colors are purple, pink, and white.

Another way to accentuate the vertical is to use plants with swordlike leaves to contrast with all the mounds and trailers in the plant world. Linear, upright leaves bring vigor and excitement to container plantings. Placing dracaena (*Cordyline indivisa*) in the middle of a pot may be a cliché, but it still works. The narrow, stiff to slightly arching blades fan out from the center like fireworks. More glamorous New Zealand flax (*Phormium* spp.) has a similar form but is an altogether bigger, bolder plant with broader leaves, which come in gorgeous colors, including solid bronze, red-purple, and olive green striped with salmon pink. Initially expensive but easy to overwinter, phormiums are undemanding and will tolerate both sun and shade.

Foliage plants come into their own in the container

BELOW AND RIGHT: Cleopatra's charms could not rival those of the genus *Solenostemon* with their infinite variety.

OPPOSITE TOP: Begonia 'Nonstop Pink,' with the decorative foliage of a cane begonia, 'Little Brother Montgomery,' and coleus.

OPPOSITE BOTTOM: New Guinea impatiens 'Fuchsia on Lavender' brings pizzazz to the partnership with variegated sweet potato vine, *Ipomoea batatas* 'Pink Frost.'

garden, providing long-term color and substance on which you can depend — and coleus is one of the best of the best. Rising above the burdensome new name of *Solenostemon*, this plant offers an array of colors and patterns that truly boggle the mind. They run the gamut from jazzy combinations of yellow, dark red, and lime green to subtle medleys of khaki, olive green, and maroon. The solid colors also offer a tremendous range of hues from stinging yellow-green to muted bronze to rich, saturated shades of red and purple.

The most familiar leaf shape, a simple, pointed ellipse with toothed edges, gives coleus one of its common names, painted nettle, but there are also forms with lobed, scalloped, or frilled edges, and all these styles come in different sizes. The plant habit varies from semitrailing to bushy with a three-foot spread. A large, full specimen can play the major part in a mixed planting or act as a "shrub" to counterbalance tall plants such as canna or elephant's ear.

While it would be a mistake to bill coleus as a shade lover — sun brings out the best in all the colors, especially the brightest hues — nevertheless the plant itself will grow perfectly well in low-light situations. Coleus cultivars thrive on Kate Resek's rooftop and put on a fine display. The worst that can happen in the shade is that the yellows will become greener and the reds and purples less vibrant, but if you experiment, you are sure to come up with some that are satisfactory.

Caladiums, on the other hand, are bona fide shade lovers and have the candlepower to light up a dark garden. Their large but paper-thin leaves come in lovely pale blends of pink, green, and white and also an eye-catching pure white with green veining as well as brighter bicolor combinations of green and white, pink and green, and red and green. Native to Central America and related to calla lilies, caladiums prefer the kind of shade found in city gardens, where reflected light brightens the atmosphere, but they will do well even in deep shade.

With the leaves of caladiums and the flowers of begonias, you can't feel cheated of color in a shady garden. Large-flowered tuberous begonias have a color range that includes red, orange, yellow, pink, salmon, and white. The blossoms, both double (the male flowers) and single (the females), are gorgeous and appear at the same time. And the shiny, dark green foliage sets them off to sleek perfection. You can't go wrong with the so-called Nonstop series, which offers all the colors, and they really live up to their promise of continual bloom.

Other begonias that perform well in shade include cane, or angel-wing, begonias, which have fibrous roots (as opposed to tubers), beautiful leaves — sometimes decorated with silver spots or stippled patterns — and drooping sprays of small flowers. Some by virtue of their form and flowers are good candidates for hanging baskets; others are upright in habit. The toughest and most tolerant of all begonias have to be the little annual wax begonias (*Begonia semperflorens-cultorum*), with either green or bronze foliage. In sun or shade, the small, flat-faced flowers bloom no matter what.

Few other flowering annuals actively like shade, with the striking exception of impatiens (*Impatiens walleriana*), the hands-down winner for producing color in the darkest garden. And what a range of hues! Red, mauve, magenta, pink, salmon, rose, and orange. Impatiens also comes in pure white and white with candy-cane stripes in magenta, red, and pink. Common garden impatiens are native to west Africa, while New Guinea impatiens hails, as one might expect, from New Guinea and the Solomon Islands. A comparative newcomer, this more robust impatiens produces many flowers — up to three inches across — in the same color range as *I. walleriana*. But the big news is the foliage, which is either a rich, dark green or spectacularly variegated in yellow, red, pink, and bronze. To perform their best, they need more light than their common cousins and will even grow in full sun if they are watered regularly and generously.

If your shady garden receives a few hours of sun, it is worth trying petunias. They bloom over a long period, produce a multitude of flowers, and are suitable for either mingling with other plants or cascading down from planters and hanging baskets. Petunias are generally divided into multifloras and grandifloras. The many-flowered smaller blossoms hold up best and require the least

In Kate Resek's cool, shady garden, caladium creates a hot spot with its vivid cerise leaves bordered in green.

OPPOSITE: Common impatiens (background) and petunias (center) have always been container classics prized for their colorful flowers and ease of culture.

Petunias and nicotianas at the New York Botanical Garden.

attention. Grandifloras have the biggest flowers but are messy and look a perfect wreck after rain. I'm fondest of the species *Petunia integrifolia*, which has magenta flowers no bigger than a quarter, and the tiny petunia look-alike, *Callibracoa*, or "million bells."

Tobacco plant (*Nicotiana*) is a petunia relative that will also tolerate some shade. My father loved the rangy old-fashioned kind, *Nicotiana alata*. He always planted it next to the house, where we could smell its perfume in the evening. The long tube of the corolla opens into a white star-faced flower, which droops during the day and rights itself late in the afternoon, pouring forth its heavenly scent to attract nocturnal pollinators. New cultivars of this plant are shorter, about two and a half feet tall, remain fully open during the day, and come in many attractive colors: shades and tints of pink, deep red, light violet, lime green, and, of course, white. However, these improvements have been wrought at the expense of the lovely scent.

Among the tender perennials, no list of mainstays would be complete without the indispensable zonal geraniums (*Pelargonium* x *hortorum*), so called because their leaves often sport "zones" of different colors. For instance, the leaves of 'A Happy Thought' are quite startling, with lemon yellow centers and green edges. The flower clusters are cherry red and of a modest size. 'Crystal Palace Gem' has chartreuse leaves with green centers and small, loose clusters of orange-red flowers. Ordinary geraniums with big, solid flower heads and green leaves, which may or may not have a suggestion of a darker zone, are too familiar to require further description. Suffice it to say that those flowers, in red, pink, salmon, orange, or white, really pack a wallop, and the plants themselves are good for the long haul. In addition to the zonal geraniums, some of the scented varieties, with modest to nondescript

flowers, offer instead extremely attractive green, gray-green, and variegated leaves.

Although the Australian fan flower (*Scaevola aemula*) only appeared on the scene about a dozen years ago, it is now considered a mainstay for hanging baskets and in mixed containers as a semitrailing ground cover. The plants are about ten inches tall, with flat clusters of violet flowers at the tips of the branches, which elongate as the season progresses. Each flower has five fingers spread open like a tiny fan, hence the name. They flower without pause all season and well into the fall (see photo top right on page 70).

Vines, with their highs and lows, their ups and downs, tie the container garden together — literally and figuratively. While everybody knows and loves the well-named 'Heavenly Blue' morning glory (*Ipomoea tricolor*), another member of the family recently made

Supported by coleus and New Zealand flax, familiar but fabulous geraniums provide the flower power in this combination.

LEFT: "Zones" of chartreuse and green make the leaves of 'Crystal Palace Gem' almost as eye-catching as the flowers.

OPPOSITE: Zonal geranium 'Crystal Palace Gem' brings its bright flowers and colorful foliage to an entrance on my terrace.

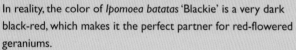

In reality, the color of *Ipomoea batatas* 'Blackie' is a very dark black-red, which makes it the perfect partner for red-flowered geraniums.

TOP RIGHT: *I. batatas* 'Ace of Spades,' a newer cultivar with an interesting shape, mingles here with Australian fan flower.

BOTTOM RIGHT: Pastel 'Pink Frost' goes superbly with pinks and purples. It is a more delicate member of the same family, *I. batatas*, with stems only two or three feet long.

it big among container gardeners. All of us are crazy about sweet potato vine (*I. batatas*) in its many colorful forms, which trail rather than climb. 'Blackie,' a cultivar with sooty leaves divided into three pointed lobes, pours from tubs and window boxes everywhere. Meanwhile, adventurous gardeners are seeking out 'Ace of Spades,' with foliage color and form to match its name. On the light side, we have 'Pink Frost,' with small, pointed leaves variegated in tints of pink and green, and on the bright side, 'Margarita,' with chartreuse leaves. These vines soften sharp edges and hard surfaces and tie the container garden to its site. The length of the trailing stems runs from three to six feet.

While the fortunes of sweet potato vine have waxed, those of scarlet runner bean (*Phaseolus coccineus*) have waned. But it deserves to be reinstated in container gardens. Attractive and easy to grow, it climbs to about eight feet, twining eagerly around poles and twig structures, and bears upright sprays of orange-red pealike flowers. An old-fashioned cultivar called 'Painted Lady' has pretty two-toned pink flowers. The pods of both are delicious to eat if picked young. Older pods become rough and slightly hairy.

The cup-and-saucer vine (*Cobaea scandens*) is one of my true loves. Its greenish white or purple flowers are attractive and interesting in shape, like large, full Canterbury bells attached to green saucerlike calyxes. The vine itself is a quick study, ascending rapidly by fragile-looking but determined tendrils that can grip

'Margarita,' a vigorous grower, cascades down from a container on Steve Silk's patio, covering the flagstones with vivid chartreuse leaves.

TOP: A strong enthusiastic climber that can quickly cover a trellis, the cup-and-saucer vine is also called monastery bells.

BOTTOM: The lacy dark green foliage and bright flowers of 'Lemon Gem' marigolds stand out against the large yellow-green *Ipomoea batatas* 'Margarita.'

OPPOSITE: 'Profusion Orange' zinnias in the foreground of a tropical border.

anything. This is the plant that enveloped my husband's espaliered pear tree in its first year in the garden. More recently, a cultivar called 'Key Lime' covered the entrance arch with its greenish white flowers and fine dark green foliage.

All the vines mentioned require sun, but a small, delicate member of the nasturtium family, canary creeper (*Tropaeolum peregrinum*), will tolerate quite a bit of shade and actively likes afternoon shade. The canary creeper is a dainty six- to ten-foot vine with small lobed leaves and charming yellow fringed flowers.

True annuals for the container garden are so numerous and common that I'm only going to suggest a couple of the more unusual ones that Steve and I have particularly enjoyed. Of course, everyone is familiar with cute, chunky little dwarf French marigolds (*Tagetes patula*). I love them myself, but Steve is a great champion of the so-called 'Gem series,' developed from *T. tenuifolia*. "They create a twelve-inch dome of ferny foliage topped with a crowd of starry little flowers about a quarter of the size of a regular marigold and of rather more subtle coloration. My favorite is lemon yellow 'Lemon Gem.' "

You must also try *Zinnia angustifolia*, another small, less common member of a very well-known family. Its growth habit is vigorously branching from the base, and every stem is covered with narrow, mildew-resistant leaves and many, many small single flowers. Look for 'Crystal White,' 'Profusion Cherry,' and 'Profusion Orange.' All reach a foot in height. They are colorful enough to hold their own alone, but they mingle so cheerfully with other larger flowers that it's a pity not to use them in a mixed planter.

CHAPTER FOUR

Purposeful Pots

Choosing and Planting Containers

Choosing pots for a container garden is almost as much fun as choosing plants. As I've said before, there is a difference between decorating with potted plants and making a garden. *Decoration* implies the addition of something extra, an accessory. In the photograph on page 74, perfectly chosen potted plants embellish the charms of a nineteenth-century house. Plants used in this way play second fiddle to the architecture. But at the entrance to Martha Cheshire's house, they are the star turn. And there is another difference. While decoration need only be looked at, a garden must be discovered by exploration, which means

Used as decoration, with taste and restraint, potted plants complement this dignified nineteenth-century home.

OPPOSITE: On Martha Cheshire's front patio, the plants have a more active role. They surround visitors and guide them to the front door.

that the viewer has to enter into the garden space. Visitors approach the Cheshires' front door *through* a container garden.

Choosing Containers: Style and Material

It goes without saying that all of us who engage in container gardening love pots. Steve has all kinds. "I've got tall ones, short ones, clay, concrete, a few metal ones, and even an old wooden burl I drilled out so that it can accept a four-inch plastic insert. I've got blue ones, green ones, black ones, brown ones. Some are shaped like animals, others are ornamented with curlicues or berries, and some are as plain as day. I also use a ton of black plastic nursery pots, which are usually hidden behind the more attractive containers in my potted border."

This handsome terra-cotta container is simply planted with dracaena (*Cordyline indivisa*) as an accent.

OPPOSITE: Cement can be molded into almost any form and is a popular material for containers and garden ornaments. Although it is heavy, its durability and winter hardiness make it a good choice for year-round container gardens.

This cache of pots in a friend's shed amply demonstrates the charms and drawbacks of terra-cotta. The colors are lovely but clay is fragile.

OPPOSITE: An empty plastic terra-cotta look-alike awaits planting on my terrace.

Lee Anne White favors colorful ceramic pots with multihued glazes because "they serve as the basis for so many interesting color combinations." She pairs blue pots with gray foliage plants, dark green pots with plants that have variegated green and gold leaves, and burgundy red pots with sedums in soft tones of red and green.

At last count I had seventy containers. I'm attached to them all but love best the imported Italian terra-cotta pots. They are beautiful to look at and contribute to the "bone structure" of the garden with their strong shapes and solid forms. The colors are determined by the mineral content of the local soils and, depending on where the pots were made, run the gamut from dusty pink to reddish brown to burned orange. These warm, neutral hues go with all flower colors and provide a subtle contrast with cool green foliage.

However, imported terra-cotta pots are porous, fragile, and not suitable for windy rooftops. The soil dries out quickly in them because of evaporation and they break easily, as Per Rasmussen learned to his cost. "The pine tree was in a terra-cotta pot — a beautiful one with lion's head handles — I just loved it. But the tree blew over, and the pot cracked." Italian clay pots are expensive too, and for a reason. They must be packed with care, handled gingerly en route, and treated with respect on arrival. Some are purported to be "frost proof," but I wouldn't leave one outside in the winter full of earth. When damp soil freezes, it expands enough to crack pottery. I empty my breakable pots at the end of the season and store them in the cellar.

To own an antique stone sink from England is every American container gardener's dream, but they are hard to come by, very expensive, and weigh hundreds of pounds. Therefore, we should not turn up our noses at cement, a fluid material that can be cast in a variety of forms, costs comparatively little, and ages gracefully. In addition, cement containers are winter hardy and provide excellent insulation for plant roots. But they are heavy and, therefore, not appropriate for balconies and some rooftop gardens.

Cement is one of the chief ingredients in hypertufa, a stone substitute that can be mixed at home and fashioned into either free-form containers or any simple round, square, or rectangular shape you fancy. Mary Stambaugh first met simulated stone troughs at a rock gardening conference in Washington State, where she acquired the original recipe. Today she uses a modified version based on the recipe in H. Lincoln Foster's book *Rock Gardening*, which you will find on page 80.

Plastic pots that look like stone or terra-cotta are a boon to rooftop gardeners and a blessing to all container gardeners. I have collected quite a few, and they are a godsend. Tough, weatherproof, and lightweight, the best ones can easily pass for the real thing and have several advantages. In the summer, plants growing in plastic containers need less water than plants growing in porous clay, and in the winter the containers can be safely left outside full of earth because plastic is flexible enough to give when the soil freezes.

Fiberglass, which is made from fine glass filaments, has the same virtues as plastic. Besides being feather-weight and strong, it can be molded and pressed into beautiful, sharply detailed designs. Eighteen years ago I

MAKING YOUR OWN STONE CONTAINERS

Dump the ingredients listed below into a large wheelbarrow and stir with a steel rake until very thoroughly combined. (Shredded nylon fiber, available where building supplies are sold, comes in premeasured three-ounce bags, approximately one cup. One three-ounce bag will reinforce three hundred pounds of concrete.)

> 1 part portland cement
> 1 1/2 parts shredded sphagnum peat moss
> 1 1/2 parts agricultural perlite
> small amount of shredded nylon fiber

One of Mary Stambaugh's homemade "stone" pots welcomes visitors at the entrance to her container garden and provides a year-round home for an Alberta spruce.

Begin slowly adding water with a hose, stirring and mixing vigorously. This is hard work and requires both stamina and elbow grease. The mixture should be the consistency of dough, soft enough to handle but not sloppy. For the form, use a plastic bowl, wastebasket, hamper, or whatever you like. Turn the form upside down on a sheet of plywood and start patting the dough onto the bottom. Work your way down the sides. The bottom and the side walls should be two to three inches thick. While the dough is still malleable, stick short lengths of half-inch dowel in the bottom for drainage holes. After the pot is dry, you can remove the dowels and make holes in the plastic liner with a hand drill.

Roughing up the surface with a wire brush before it is completely dry gives the simulated stone a weathered look. If there are too many nylon "whiskers" sticking out, burn them off with a kitchen match. Although these homemade containers do not weigh as much as real stone, they are not light either. It took two strong men and a pickup truck to bring my biggest container from Mary's potting shed, where I made it, to our back door, where it has been ever since.

was given a gray fiberglass basket that looks remarkably like stone, but empty, it can be lifted with one finger. This container has spent its entire life outside and is none the worse for wear. Initially expensive, fiberglass containers are even more durable than their plastic counterparts.

Wood is a deservedly popular material for window boxes, planters, screens, fences, and outdoor furniture. It is sturdy and relatively light in weight and can be painted or stained any color. Rot-resistant woods, such as white cedar and redwood, can be left untreated and will weather to a silver-gray tone that goes with all flower and foliage colors. And lest we forget, oak whiskey barrels sawn in half make commodious, long-lived containers for a rustic garden. I have several that have been in constant use for years. At the time I bought them, they cost fifteen dollars apiece, and although they've doubled in price, they're still a bargain.

Finally, you can fashion your own container from virtually anything that will hold soil, as author Rebecca Cole is eager to show you in *Potted Gardens*. She takes an old red fire bucket and leads you through every step, from banging drainage holes in the bottom

TOP: On my terrace wall, ivy geraniums drape the edge of a wooden "clam hod" painted Monet green and provided with a twisted vine for the handle.

BOTTOM: This wicker basket, used as a wall container, has a black plastic liner with drainage holes punched in the bottom to allow the excess water to escape.

A ten-by-twenty-four-inch window box planted with four wax begonias, two angelonias, and two Swedish ivies on my terrace wall.

OPPOSITE: Coleus in a flared pot twelve by nine inches (foreground left); dahlia 'Fascination' with an ultimate height of three feet and a spread of eighteen inches in a thirteen-by-fifteen-inch pot (foreground right); elephant's ear in a twenty-by-sixteen-inch pot (background center).

with a pickax to putting curved shards of broken flower-pot over the holes — curved side up — to keep the potting mix in and allow the excess water to flow out.

Drainage is the most important thing to keep in mind if you are using a nonconventional container. You must provide enough holes to release any water that is not absorbed by the planting medium. Altern-atively, if you find an interesting artifact — such as a slatted orange crate or a wicker basket — that has too many holes, you can line it with heavy black plastic, then poke holes in the plastic.

Matching Plant to Pot

Once you've picked out a number of containers, you are ready to start planting. Basically you have two choices. You can pot up your plants individually and create a group composition with them, or you can mix and match plants in a single container. Naturally, if you are going to combine several plants in one pot, it should be big enough to accommodate them all. Although there is no strict ratio of plant size to pot size, you should have some idea of how much the plants will grow in a season and match the plant to the pot. To guide you, most nurs-ery labels give approximate dimensions for the full-grown plant, be it annual, perennial, shrub, or tree.

As a rule of thumb, I've found that a single bushy specimen of coleus, flowering maple, or fuchsia will fill a pot twelve inches in diameter and nine or ten inches deep. For single specimens of strapping tropi-cal plants, cannas, and brugmansias, go for the largest pots you can find. Although my biggest pots are eigh-teen inches deep and a generous twenty-four inches across, the same diameter as most half whiskey bar-rels, the brugmansia roots always find their way out through the drainage holes by the end of the season.

This brugmansia cutting has filled its temporary pot with roots and is ready to be planted in its permanent eighteen-by-twenty-four-inch container.

OPPOSITE: Succulents and cacti from arid climates require special soils containing a high proportion of coarse sand and grit to ensure rapid drainage.

On the whole, it makes sense to use a big pot for a big plant, a small pot for a small plant. However, early in the season, before potentially large plants have hit their stride, it is a good idea to pot them in nursery containers suited to their immature size and move them to their permanent homes after the roots have filled their interim pots. The reason for this extra step is that a large volume of soil stores more water than a small plant can use. As a result, the plant may rot.

For a mixed planting, a sixteen-inch- to twenty-inch-diameter pot or a fourteen-inch-square planter provides enough room for three robust coleus plants, which can mature to two feet in every direction, plus a trailer or two and an upright centerpiece. And a ten-by-twenty-four-inch window box will easily accommodate four dwarf French marigolds or wax begonias, with room for two or three tall plants in the center and ivies or other trailing plants tucked in among them. Heretical as this may sound, you will find that if potted plants are well fed and well watered, they will tolerate considerable crowding.

Take note, however, that the plants mentioned so far have been annuals or tender perennials. Hardy perennials, shrubs, and trees are less forgiving of cramped quarters. Four-season container gardeners should heed Linda Yang's advice in *The City Gardener's Handbook*. She recommends minimum dimensions of fourteen inches in length, width, and depth for any plant that will spend the winter outdoors in Zones 6 and 7. Plants growing in containers are exposed to the weather on all sides. For this reason, their roots need as much soil around them as possible to protect them from the cold. As a further precaution, select trees, shrubs, and perennials that have a hardiness rating of at least one zone colder than the zone in which you garden. This means that if you live in Zone 6 or 7, you should look for plants that are hardy at least to Zones 5 and 6, respectively.

Potting Soils

For a container garden, the best planting medium is not soil from the garden, which is too heavy and compact for potted plants, but specially formulated potting mixes available at nurseries and garden centers. You can also mix your own using a combination of peat moss, compost — bagged or homemade — and sand. A good potting mix must strike a happy balance between water retention and drainage. As plant roots need both water and air, the soil must contain enough spongy organic matter to absorb and hold water and enough drainage material to allow the excess to escape quickly. Standing water is a death sentence to potted plants. To make sure that your potting soil meets the rapid drainage requirement, fill a small container with the mix and water it. The excess water should begin to drip out of the bottom within a few seconds.

In addition to peat moss, humus, and sand, commercial potting soils usually contain little pellets of perlite, derived from sterile volcanic rock, to lighten the mix. The combination of all these ingredients guarantees good water retention and speedy drainage. The brand I like best is Fafard. The Fafard company owns and operates peat bogs in Canada and has been formulating potting soils for seventy-five years. In addition to their regular all-purpose mix, they make a lighter-weight soil specifically designed for containers, and an even lighter, grittier mix for growing cacti.

Lee Anne White uses either Fafard or Pro-Mix combined with bagged compost. "Compost composes at least a third of the total mix," she says. "I add several bags of compost to one bale of either Pro-Mix or Fafard, depending on what I can find, mix them in a large wheelbarrow, and fill the pots from there."

Steve also uses Pro-Mix: "To a wheelbarrow load of Pro-Mix, I add a couple of shovelfuls each of sand, compost, and bark to get that classic 'fast-draining but moisture-retentive soil' you read about. The sand and bark help it to drain, and the composty stuff adds slow-release nutrients and retains moisture."

If you have your own basic formula, you can always tailor the proportions of peat, compost, and sand to suit your favorite plants. Add more sand and gravel to speed up drainage for desert plants and more organic matter — peat moss or compost — for leafy tropicals, which require a lot of moisture.

Planting the Containers

The actual planting is the best part, but messy. Unless you have the luxury of a potting area, you will want to assemble your pots, plants, and soil on a tarpaulin. To prepare the containers, put either a curved shard of broken pot, à la *Potted Gardens*, or a piece of window screen over the drainage holes to keep the soil from escaping. I find screen, which you can buy by the foot at the hardware store, works best. I used to put a layer of pebbles or bark mulch in the bottom of the pots before filling them with soil, and many container gardeners still do it, but it isn't necessary.

Fill the prepared container half full of potting soil and tamp it down gently. To remove plants from their nursery pots, cover the top of the pot with your hand — fingers spread apart on either side of the stem or stems — tip the pot upside down, and tap the

An early planting session is in full swing. Before you begin planting, spread a tarp and assemble your supplies: plants, potting soil, and containers. Have the hose or a watering can ready — and enjoy!

OPPOSITE: A potting mix heavy on moisture-retaining organic matter suits large-leaved, water-loving tropical plants, like this elephant's ear.

Freeing the roots of a potted dracaena before planting encourages them to grow outward into the soil.

Adding finishing touches to one of the matched pots flanking the gateway to the garden.

Each pot has dracaena as the centerpiece, surrounded by tall, pink angelonias; *Fuchsia* 'Rose Beacon' provides substance, and ivies, the grace notes.

bottom. The plant, with the soil intact, should come out in your hand. If the roots have completely filled the pot and are tightly intertwined, free them up a bit before setting the plant or plants on the base of potting soil.

Having set your plants, add potting soil and gently firm it around them. When you are finished, the soil level in relation to the plant should be no higher than it was in the nursery pot and about an inch below the top of the new container. I plant mixed containers in the following order: the tall centerpiece first, then the large plants around it. Next tuck in a filler or two, if there is room, and squeeze in a couple of trailing plants last. The final step is to water carefully but thoroughly, using a hose or watering can equipped with a rose attachment that delivers a soft flow of water.

OPPOSITE: With lesser pots clustered at their feet, these large pots give special emphasis to the central opening in the terrace wall.

CHAPTER FIVE

Putting It All Together

Arranging Containers

Now that you have all of these wonderful plants potted up, what next? If you have planted each one in a separate container, then you are ready to start making your garden. But if you are embarking on a mixed planting, here are a few design tips. You need a point of concentration and focus, a centerpiece that will become about twice the height of the container and give your composition upward thrust. And for balance, you need a couple of substantial plants to hold it all down. These should have either showy flowers or bold, decorative leaves or both. If there is room, you might want to add an airy filler, and to soften the hard rim of the pot, a vinelike

With all the pieces in place, the terrace soon begins to look like a garden.

OPPOSITE: Canna 'Tropicanna' and dahlias provide the thriller, coleus serves as a filler, and wispy variegated Saint Augustine grass spills over the edge.

Clusters of potted plants are the building blocks of a container garden.

A group of four pots with a spiky centerpiece introduces two strong, upright forms that contrast with the flat plane of the patio.

On this terrace, flue tiles surrounding a handsome agave lead visitors to French doors.

And here, a more elaborate collection of potted plants creates interest against a wall.

plant to trail over the edge. As Steve puts it, you need "a thriller (showy flowers or foliage), a filler (small foliage and/or flowers), and a spiller."

The Building Blocks

Potted plants are the raw materials from which container gardens are made, and clusters or groups of pots are the building blocks. They can be used to create structure, divide space, direct traffic, define boundaries, and more. Like a mixed container, a cluster of pots resembles a planetary system with a prominent "sun" surrounded by supporting stars. For informal groupings, odd numbers seem to work best. But these arrangements can involve as many or as few as you want and may be of any size or configuration. The photographs on this page show three clusters of potted plants, each used in a different way. In one, a simple arrangement of four containers, with spiky cordyline as the sun, adds drama to a patio and links it to its garden setting. In another, a galaxy of hexagonal flue tiles orbits an agave raised on a tall cylinder used to lead the way to French doors. And in the third, a complex frieze of potted plants with an ornamental grass as the background and high point enlivens an otherwise blank wall.

Organizing Space

At this point the born planners among you may want to go out and buy a pad of graph paper and draw to scale an outline of your patio, deck, or rooftop. If that idea appeals to you, the next step is to cut out lots of little circles, squares, and rectangles, using the same scale, to represent your pots and planters. Now you can try different groupings by sliding the pieces around your checkerboard. But if you are like most of the container

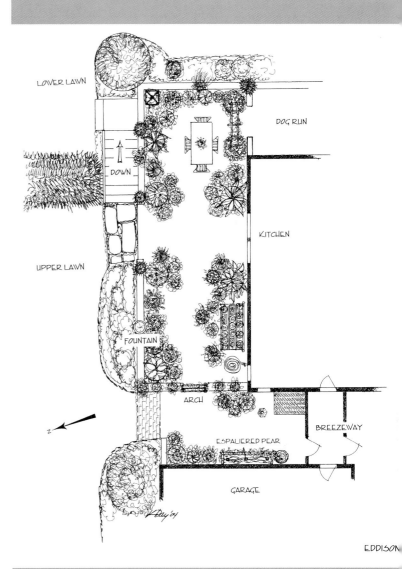

EDDISON

gardeners I know, and like every gardener in this book, you will prefer to go outside and bodily shove your containers around until you're happy with their arrangement.

However, as design is about making the most of space, seeing plans may help you get your bearings. The plans were created by graphic artist Kim Proctor *after* the contributors had arrived at the design of their gardens. Each gardener provided Kim with measurements and rough sketches, and she drew up the plans. Meanwhile, all of us had already had the fun of arranging and rearranging our containers.

Now that you have seen the plan of my terrace, let me take you on a virtual tour of my garden. Come through the breezeway, past my husband's espaliered

Visitors enter the container garden from the breezeway end of the terrace through the arch.

A path threads its way through the potted plants to a separate dining area in a clearing at the far end.

From the dining table you can look out at the perennial beds or back toward the arch.

Alocasia with a foreground of coleus fills one outside corner.

RIGHT: And a pair of arborvitae, backed up by symmetrical groups of pots on either side of the center opening, frame a view of the perennial gardens.

OPPOSITE: A tuteur covered with pink-flowered mandevilla addresses the opposite outside corner.

pear tree, and turn right under the arch. Avert your eyes from the untidily coiled hose on your right and proceed to the middle of the terrace. When you arrive, you will be opposite the sliding doors to the kitchen and the center opening in the terrace wall. A few more steps and you can sit at the table and look out either toward the perennial borders or back toward the arch. You may catch a glimpse of the dog run disguised by the vine-covered trellis, but I hope you won't.

That is all there is to my container garden: a narrow rectangle thirty-three feet long and twelve feet wide, surrounded by a low brick wall with three openings in it. The challenge is to make it look different every year by designing a new "set," complete with new plants and a different color scheme. But like any stage, the site has limitations. Its size and shape and the position of the openings are fixed, and the breezeway end,

which provides access to and from the garage, remains a passageway. A lengthwise path down the middle of the terrace made sense in practical terms but lacked interest. So instead, the path curves around clusters of potted plants, which separate the space into a "foyer" and a "dining room."

Structure

To give the container garden a bit of structure, I start every season by addressing the outside corners and creating a sense of enclosure. For these important corner spots, I use either large architectural plants with impressive foliage — such as alocasias or cannas in suitably proportioned containers — or tall, narrow vine-clad pyramids set in half whiskey barrels.

Next I think about the entrances. Sometimes my two

TOP: Per Rasmussen's rooftop terrace boasts a breathtaking view to the east, where the lights of New York City have already begun to glitter in the twilight.

BOTTOM: The view from the living room doors looking south is less dramatic but no less pleasing. In the early evening light, the fountain, flanked by geraniums, stands out against the dark background of the hedge.

OPPOSITE: In this daytime view from the center garden, a billowing green landscape of treetops conceals the busy streets below.

Mexican pottery chickens perch on top of the wall, facing each other across the center opening, but without backup, they are not big enough to hold their own. It takes the addition of large containers, one on either side, surrounded by smaller pots to help frame the view.

Once the corners have been filled and the entrances framed, I tackle the north wall of the kitchen, which is the backdrop for the container garden. Except for the sliding doors and a small kitchen window, the expanse of clapboard is unbroken and uninteresting. I usually station treelike brugmansias, planted in twenty-by-twenty-four-inch pots, on either side of the sliding doors to break up the space with their leafy crowns and huge apricot orange flowers. But this year they were banished to the back-door entryway because they didn't fit into the cool mauve, purple, and pink color scheme. Instead, I had to rely on a trellis to relieve the monotony of the clapboard wall.

Dividing a Large Space

Dividing and conquering a thirty-three-by-twelve-foot space like mine is one thing. Orchestrating a sixty-five-by-thirty-five-foot rooftop terrace into three separate garden rooms is quite another. Not surprisingly, it took Per Rasmussen several seasons to arrive at the layout you now see. "When I first started working on the garden," says Per, "the gazebo and shed weren't here. The terrace was completely empty and open to the sky. I knew that such a big space should be broken up in some way and that it needed a focal point to draw your eye across the terrace. So I grouped the trees in the middle, but that didn't work. They were too tall and kept getting blown down by the wind. Moreover, they blocked the view."

To restore the spectacular cityscape to the east and the treetops of New Jersey to the south and west, Per banished the tallest evergreens to the corners of the terrace and deployed the others at intervals around the perimeter. Within this framework, he put to the test different subdivisions of the remaining space. When the gazebo and tool shed were added, they changed the shape of the terrace. Centered on the living room doors, the new overhead structure provided much-needed shade and made the space beneath its roof more intimate and manageable for entertaining. It also gave Per a starting point for the first of three separate garden rooms.

Looking south from the living room doors, he imagined a garden room with a little fountain at the far end as the central feature. But once he had installed the fountain, he realized that it needed a background. He provided this with a juniper hedge punctuated at each end by tall arborvitae, and for color, window boxes full of geraniums.

With his training in art and architecture, Per was better equipped than most gardeners to tackle major design projects like the gazebo and tool shed. But he found that developing the gardens took longer than ex-

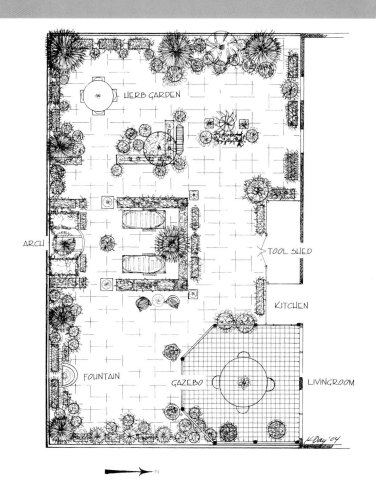

RASMUSSEN

pected. He wanted to use hardy perennials, trees, and shrubs as well as annuals and tender perennials, so that there would be something to look at year-round. But this meant learning, by trial and error, which species could take the exposed situation in the winter. Meanwhile, he continued to experiment with groupings of containers, combining them with ornaments, furniture, and architectural fragments to serve as partitions between the garden rooms.

He tried several different layouts for the small garden in the middle of the terrace and finally settled on an arrangement of wooden planters forming three sides of a rectangle. A cedar, grown as a standard and pruned into an umbrella shape, now provides the

The herb garden in the southwest corner of the terrace offers outdoor dining and a fine view.

RIGHT: Nearby, tomatoes for the table share a planter with marigolds.

OPPOSITE: In Kate Resek's small city garden, the glimpse of sky between buildings creates a sense of space and distance.

centerpiece, and two lounge chairs, one on each side of the cedar, face a soaring archway of white metal tubing that was once a stage prop. "It's wonderful here at night," says Per. "If you look through the arch, you can see all the bridges lit up like necklaces. It's a whole different look at night."

The last room to take shape was the square herb garden in the southwest corner, set apart from the rest of the terrace by planters and sections of balustrade. The architectural elements are low enough to afford the garden its full share of the distant panorama but distinctive enough to give it a character of its own. Within the enclosure a round table and four chairs await diners. And at the foot of the parapet, pots of lavender and deep window boxes full of culinary herbs, salad greens, and tomatoes alternate with large containers of evergreens.

Making Less More

While Per managed to turn a vast exposed rooftop into a spectacular container garden with rooms and a view, Kate Resek worked a different kind of magic with a

small, enclosed space. As her apartment is only one flight up from the constant noise and activity of New York City, she wanted to buffer herself from that world and keep her focus within the garden, at the same time preserving a narrow vista to the west.

To lighten the stern facades of adjacent buildings, she had diamond-patterned lattice, which takes up no floor space, attached to the walls on three sides, leaving the far end open. Above the rhododendrons, which form the fourth wall, a sliver of sky, crosshatched with skeletal fire escapes, affords a sense of distance. Within this airy enclosure, Kate has arranged a greenbelt of small ornamental trees and evergreens to provide privacy and a background for her flowering annuals and colorful foliage plants.

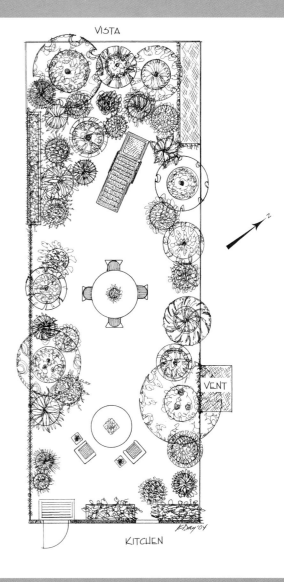

In the center of the leafy oasis, there is room for a chaise longue, wrought metal dining set, and near the kitchen door, two comfortable chairs. Sitting here on a summer afternoon, hedged in by old buildings and surrounded by plants, one might be in some venerable European city instead of a stone's throw from the Lexington Avenue subway.

The only modern intrusion is a four-story vent that the restaurant below was required to install on the north side of the building. To take the curse off its black bulk, Kate had vertical panels of lattice erected in front of it. A silver lace vine ascends the treillage, and in front of it, an oakleaf hydrangea with large,

Vine-covered walls, the shade of shadbush and river birch, and a pair of comfortable chairs near the back door are the making of this secret city garden.

handsome leaves provides an understory for a clump of river birch. Both of these plants offer the bonus of attractive, peeling bark, to engage the eye and draw attention to the garden rather than to its surroundings.

A successful garden is one in which the space has been used in a way that pleases the gardener. Kate wanted peace, privacy, and an outdoor place where she could enjoy her friends and family. Protected on the east by her building, owned now by the tenants, and sheltered from the gaze of neighbors by the lacy foliage of birch and shadbush, she has it all, a secret garden in the heart of the city.

In Sandy Hook, Connecticut, Alice Reisenweaver shares a secret country garden with her husband, Dennis, and an elderly beagle. The house and flagstone patio are set into a steep bank above the Pootatuck

River. Like Kate's rooftop terrace, the Reisenweaver patio is small and enclosed on all four sides. On the east a seven-foot-high retaining wall holds back the hillside, and on the west a new wooden fence, built by Dennis, screens out the sight and sound of a busy secondary road. The other two "walls" are formed by the house on the north and the garage on the south.

Alice knew what she wanted from her patio, "a comfortable, welcoming outdoor room," where she and Dennis could sit on summer evenings and cook dinner on the grill. But a room requires furniture, furniture requires room, and the kind of container garden Alice had in mind requires both. As the assistant nursery manager for a local garden center, every spring Alice orders new and fascinating plants for the garden center, only to find that she can't resist them herself. So little by little, they find their way into pots and onto her patio. But she has resolved this thorny issue by making every square inch of the fifteen-by-twenty-foot space count.

Pressing into service two narrow strips of earth — one against the garage wall, the other against the fence — she has created the illusion of deep flower borders along two sides of the patio. Ferns and other shade-tolerant perennials planted next to the garage set off a potted rainbow of annuals, tender perennials, and foliage plants at the edge of the flagstone paving. Vegetables occupy the bed against the fence, separated from the patio by a "hedge" of window boxes filled with marigolds, zinnias, and other summer flowers. In the fall these are replaced by evergreen boughs for winter decoration.

To accommodate the staggering number of plants she brings home from work or raises from seed every year, Alice has found ingenious ways of getting extra mileage out of vertical spaces. She suspends hanging baskets from the garage roof, attaches pots to the fence,

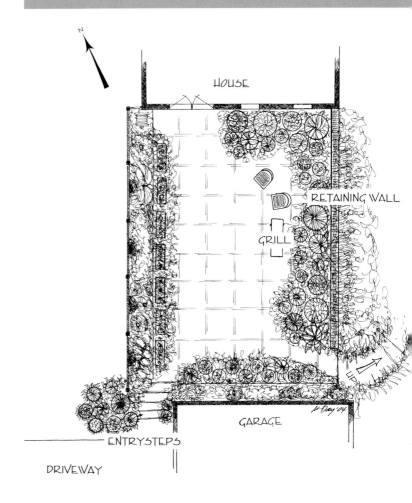

HOUSE

RETAINING WALL

GRILL

ENTRYSTEPS

DRIVEWAY

GARAGE

K Day '04

REISENWEAVER

Massed annuals and tender perennials in scintillating colors stand out against a background of ferns growing in the ground along the garage wall.

A "hedge" of marigolds planted in window boxes keeps the Reisenweaver beagle out of the vegetable garden along the fence.

A waterfall of flowers and colorful foliage pours down the steps carved into the hillside.

and urges container-grown cucumbers to scramble up the ivy-covered retaining wall. Another space-saving Reisenweaver ploy is to use all the steps to showcase plants. Visitors approaching from the driveway enter between banks of potted plants on either side of the front steps. More pots overflowing with flowers and foliage turn the steep stairs from the upper level of the property into a waterfall of color.

Tucked out of the way among the plants, lightweight, stackable dark green plastic furniture provides all that is necessary for comfortable outdoor living. "In the early spring before it gets too hot, we sit out here a lot," says Alice. "And in the summer, we barbecue almost every evening. Barbecuing is a big thing. It's nice and private for us and also for entertaining. Two or three times a year, we have parties outside on the patio and around the yard."

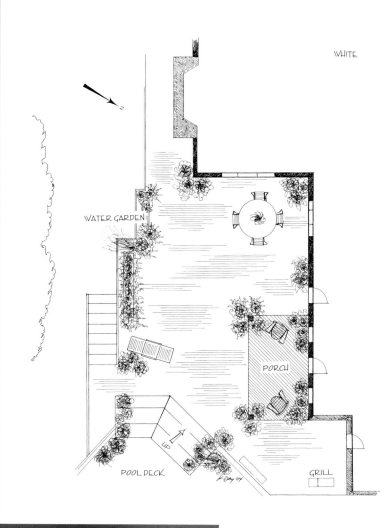

Handling Asymmetrical Spaces

As summers in Georgia are usually too hot for outdoor dining, Lee Anne White and her husband, Alan, rarely use their deck, except as the quickest route to the pool. "But," says Lee Anne, "we use it a tremendous amount in the spring and fall. In March, April, and May, we eat almost every dinner there, and often I'll go out in the morning and have my coffee or sit there and make my phone calls."

Wood being the obliging material that it is, a deck can be any shape. However, Lee Anne sees this as a drawback. Their deck, which was fitted around the

In another corner of this spacious deck, four matching chairs surround a teak dining table.

OPPOSITE: Lee Anne White's covered porch brings cooling shade to a pair of Adirondack chairs, which overlook the water garden. The focal point is provided by a red Abyssinian banana in front of a tall, airy clump of bamboo.

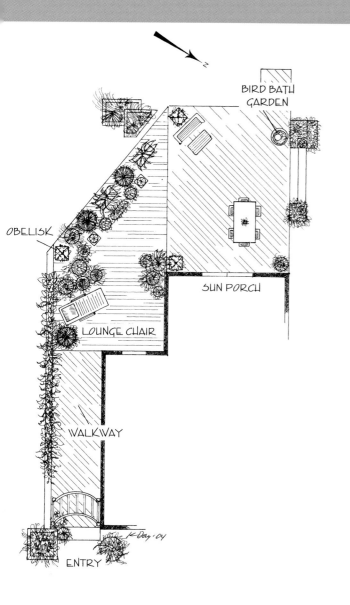

BIRD BATH GARDEN

OBELISK

SUN PORCH

LOUNGE CHAIR

WALKWAY

ENTRY

NICKEL

rambling house, has whimsical angles, wasted spaces, and awkward corners. To overcome these quirks, she disguises the defects with lush tropicals, banks the perimeter with ornamental grasses, and groups plants with bold foliage at the access points. "Although I would never design a deck like this," she says, "the odd shape, along with the groupings of pots, helps divide the space into four distinct rooms: the roofed section, where we have a pair of Adirondack chairs; the dining area; my husband's grilling area; and the open stretch that serves as a sort of passageway."

Lee Anne and Alan's deck was already a fait accompli when they bought the house, but Jan and Dave Nickel of Avon, Connecticut, started from scratch. First they worked on the house; then, using recycled lumber, they built the deck. Angular in design and covering approximately eight hundred square feet, it provides Jan, who is a plantaholic and works in a nursery, with more than enough room and endless opportunities for using plants.

The asymmetrical plan features an arbor entrance, made inviting with urns of foliage plants. From the arbor, a walkway runs along the south side of the house leading to the deck. The railing has built-in planters, which fairly bristle with vegetation. Where the deck and walkway meet, a narrow, shapely arborvitae marks the spot. A matching arborvitae, along with a four-sided metal obelisk surrounded by plants, calls attention to the corner where the deck changes direction.

While the Nickels' woodland setting has been allowed to remain semiwild, Jan has treated the deck like a room, using sheared evergreens and rusted steel structures as walls. "I wanted to give the deck a different look," she says. "And I've always admired European gardens with all those conical shrubs. That's why I keep the arborvitae tightly trimmed and use so

A collection of potted plants massed around a four-sided metal structure draws attention to a turning point in the deck, and evergreens in pots and planters provide boundary walls.

BELOW: An admirer of European gardens, Jan Nickel gives her deck a bit of formality with a symmetrical arrangement of evergreens centered on a garden ornament.

many verticals. My idea is to combine the formal and the informal — the architectural and the naturalistic."

Bringing Order to Informal Spaces

So far the garden sites in this chapter have been rectilinear and either closely associated with or attached to a house or apartment building. But trees, shrubs, and ground covers separate Mary Stambaugh's terrace from the house and loosen its ties to the architecture.

The semicircle of gravel, supported by its low fieldstone retaining wall, looks out across a crescent of lawn to a sloping meadow and rolling hills. In sympathy with the landscape, the loose surfacing material flows with the curves. Groups of containers define the outer rim of the terrace and suggest a low, informal "wall," which affords a sense of containment without spoiling the view.

To lead visitors from one side to the other, stepping-stones trace a meandering path across the gravel, skirting a well-placed island of pots, which invites you to pause. There are many things to look at, including a little reflecting pool that Mary made by sinking a flue tile in the ground and surrounding it with potted plants. Mats of thyme and silver dichondra creep among the stones that hide the edge of the tile and knit the pool into its setting.

It is always a treat to go to Mary's. A frequent and thoughtful hostess, she has arranged cushion-covered wicker chairs and a settee on the terrace in the shade of two old maples and provides iced tea for garden visitors on a table nearby. Informal but cohesive, this garden is a study in curves. Even the shape of the dining table and the backs of the chairs repeats the theme.

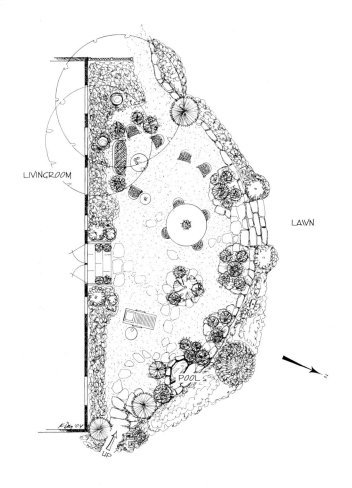

STAMBAUGH

PRECEDING PAGE: Wicker furniture provides a comfortable place to sit in the shade of an old maple tree on Mary Stambaugh's terrace.

ABOVE: Mary Stambaugh designed her terraced patio to fit into the landscape and echo the crescent shape of the lawn below.

OPPOSITE TOP: An island of pots breaks up the forty-five-by-twenty-foot Stambaugh terrace and makes the journey across it more interesting.

OPPOSITE BOTTOM: A flue tile sunk in the ground creates a convincingly natural pool, with flat stones concealing its edges.

While the shape of Mary's terrace echos the rounded forms in the landscape, Steve's patio links the house to the setting with a combination of lines and curves. Three sides of the patio agree with the straight lines of the architecture, while the fourth sweeps outward into an exuberant garden dominated by large shrubs, enormous grasses, and towering perennials. Most container displays would be dwarfed by this setting, but Steve also uses big plants in big pots on the patio.

Early in the summer, employing the architecture of the house as a background and a stunning cobalt blue trellis as a focal point, he sets up the frieze of tropical foliage and flowers that changes every year. Behind the scenes, a multilevel scaffolding of upside-down nursery pots, wooden boxes, and other supports makes the exciting, and often unlikely, plant combinations possible.

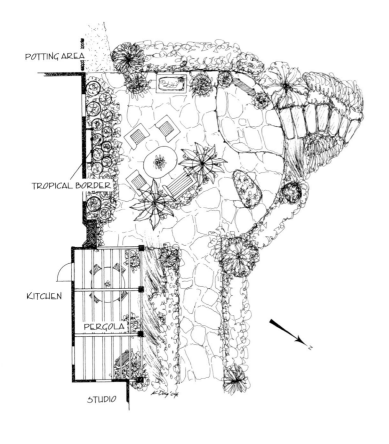

POTTING AREA

TROPICAL BORDER

KITCHEN

PERGOLA

STUDIO

SILK

A leafy garden room under the pergola ensures cool summer dining.

OPPOSITE: The pièce de résistance of Steve Silk's container garden is always the tropical border.

In an issue of *Fine Gardening* magazine, Steve let readers in on his secret: "By placing short but stellar plants atop staging that's hidden amid other plants, I can create compelling combinations that wouldn't be possible with plants grown in the ground." For instance, in order to combine the dark red leaves of the tropical smokebush (*Euphorbia cotinifolia*) with two different coleus varieties beneath a shower of red fuchsia blossoms, he had to manipulate their heights.

The smokebush is about four feet tall. The coleus are much shorter, so he set them on top of overturned flowerpots to achieve the desired effect. The fuchsia standards are about the same height as the smokebush but also required a boost in order to appear taller.

In contrast to the patio jungle, which relates to the garden and surrounding landscape, the pergola relates to the house. Leafy walls, a ceiling of vines, and curtains of trailing plants create a sense of enclosure. At the same time, these airy barriers permit glimpses of the sky, the patio, and the garden through "windows" in the herbage. Thus, the ten-by-twenty-foot concrete platform, which never made it as a greenhouse, has become instead a cool, shady room in which to enjoy summer meals.

CHAPTER SIX

Decoration

Color Schemes and Furniture

Once your container garden has a bit of bone structure, you can let yourself go and play around with color and furnishings. This is the moment to try every color scheme you've ever dreamed of. You have nothing to lose because everything is either movable or temporary, which makes a container garden the perfect place to experiment.

Color

The all-white garden at Sissinghurst Castle in Sussex, England, has been an inspiration to innumerable gardeners, myself included. But I am always reluctant to commit myself to an in-the-ground garden with such a restricted theme.

However, once I discovered container gardening, I was ready to try anything. So one summer I

In a handful of containers and an eight-foot-square entryway, I pay homage to Vita Sackville-West and the White Garden at Sissinghurst Castle in Sussex, England.

OPPOSITE: In Jan Nickel's garden you will find every nuance of green, from pure grass green to forest green, gray-green to blue-green, light, bright yellow-green to nearly black-green.

IN BRIEF: COLOR THEORY FOR GARDENERS

You will no doubt have heard that color theory is complex and wish to steer clear of the subject, but bear with me. It is the science of color that is complex, and it has become more so with advances in the fields of electricity and optics. Giant strides have been made since 1666 when Sir Isaac Newton made his breakthrough discovery that light, not pigment, is the source of color and that white light contains all the colors of the rainbow.

But color theory for artists, designers, and gardeners has remained virtually unchanged since Moses Harris, a British engraver, published the first color wheel in 1766. Like Newton before him, Harris based his theories on the order of the colors in the rainbow: red, orange, yellow, green, blue, and violet. However, what interested him most were the *relationships between colors*.

Harris arranged the colors in a circle based on "the manner in which each colour is formed" and the "harmonious connections" between colors. In short, he laid them out where they belong, according to their family relationships. Starting with red, it is logical that orange, which is "formed" by red and yellow, should be placed between its parents, and so on around the circle.

Modern color wheels, which arrange the hues in the same order and for the same reasons, are fun to use and available at any art store for under ten dollars. The Color Wheel Company in Philomath, Oregon, publishes a good one that combines show-and-tell color schemes with clear, simple explanations. Everything a gardener needs to know about color is made evident right on the color wheel.

The color wheel from Moses Harris's groundbreaking treatise *The Natural System of Colours* clearly illustrates family likenesses between related hues. It is easy to see the incremental steps between hues. Red gradually becomes less red and more like orange; orange begins to lose its red component as it approaches yellow; yellow, by degrees, cools to green; green becomes more like blue; blue like violet; and back to red.

made an all-white container garden in the eight-foot-square entryway at the back door — and I loved it. Single-hue gardens offer a fascinating challenge.

If you find the thought of sticking to one color too inhibiting, you can go to the opposite extreme and use

OPPOSITE: This tropical border sets off fireworks against the neutral gray background of the house.

the whole spectrum. This approach certainly works for Alice Reisenweaver. She stages her vivid, multihued display against green ferns and the neutral gray of the garage wall, which sets off all the colors to perfection (see page 104). The darker gray of Steve Silk's house performs a similar service for his knock-your-socks-off tropical border, while our "desert tan" clapboards provide an agreeable background for any color scheme I'm bold enough or foolish enough to try.

You are in luck if your house is painted or stained a tint, tone, or shade of gray, brown, or green. These undemanding hues flatter all colors. The terms *tint*, *tone*, and *shade* are used by artists to indicate color variations. A tint is any color diluted with white. Pink, for example, is a tint of red. A tone is a color such as sage green, which has a hint of gray in its composition. Many of our silver foliage plants are, in fact, tones of gray-green. And a shade is any color with black added. So-called black tulips are actually a very dark shade of

Closely related hues result in harmonious associations, like this one. In Steve Silk's tropical border, bloodflower creates a link with the red coleus and the deep red leaves of tropical smoke-bush (*Euphorbia cotinifolia*).

RIGHT: Red, red-orange, and orange always go well together. South American bloodflower combines all three colors in a single flower cluster.

The dramatic contrast between paired complementary colors makes them invigorating partners.

TOP LEFT: The starry flower clusters of crimson *Pentas lanceolata* and a matching coleus glow against contrasting green leaves.

TOP RIGHT: The bright yellow flowers and variegated leaves of the sunset plant (*Lysimachia congestiflora* 'Outback Sunset') intensify the purple of a browallia blossom.

BELOW: And the warm orange flowers of kalanchoe set off cool blue forget-me-nots.

red. (As artists and gardeners use color in the same way, it makes sense to share terms like *tint*, *tone*, and *shade*.)

I smile every time I hear the J. P. Morgan Chase Bank of New York commercial: "The right relationship is everything." When it comes to using color in the garden, that says it all. Understanding color relationships is the key to success. Relationships are about harmony and contrast, likenesses and differences, whether they are between a bank and its customers or between one hue and another.

In human affairs, *harmony* is based on common ground, likeness, and accord. It is the same with colors. The more alike colors are, the better they get along together. Adjacent hues on the color wheel, such as red, red-orange, and orange, share a common pigment and are always compatible. (See page 122.)

Contrast is based on difference — the attraction of opposites. Just as differences between people can result in exciting chemistry, colors that are very different from one another can also produce stimulating effects. So-called complementary colors appear opposite one another on the color wheel and are as different as colors can get. Placed side by side, complementary pairs, like red and green, yellow and violet, blue and orange, make for the highest possible contrast. In the garden, they are riveting. (See page 123.)

So there you have it. Color for gardeners is all about contrast and harmony. If you like excitement on your rooftop, deck, or patio, paired complementaries are the way to go. But if you want peace and harmony, stick to analogous color schemes. Or do what I do, chop and change every season. One year I took the primary colors — red, yellow, and blue — and put them together with their complements. The result was a cacophony of bright, contrasting colors that made some of my garden-

ing friends wince and others cheer. The next year I was inspired by a Gauguin painting and went with analogous red, orange, tangerine, straw yellow, and warm pink.

Recently I've been on a new kick, borrowing color schemes from different fabrics. A woven plaid in Arizona sunset colors gave rise to one of my favorite combinations: orange, red-orange, and golden orange with touches of mauve and shocking pink. Last year I used fresh, cheerful yellow, green, and white cotton prints, and this year a drapery fabric in cool pinks, purples, greens, and blue-greens was the point of de-

parture. The harmonious result boosted my approval rating with friends who had looked askance at complementary pairs but disappointed those who had been enthusiastic about lively contrasts and hot hues.

For me the terrace is stage, easel, and playground rolled into one. During the winter I plot, plan, and repaint the furniture. So far it has gone from white to blue to yellow to green, and who knows what's next. The wrought metal table and four chairs caught my eye a few years ago outside a secondhand shop. I liked the simple, graceful lines, and the size of the table, forty-eight inches long by thirty inches wide, was right for

On this south-facing rooftop terrace, bright flower colors hold their own in the strong sunlight.

A Gauguin-inspired color scheme with white furniture;

shades of orange in flower and foliage paired with highly contrasting blue furniture;

a symphony in sunny yellows;

cool, harmonious purples, mauves, and pinks with blue-green furniture.

our narrow terrace. The furniture's first season coincided with the Gauguin scheme, and among the hot Tahitian hues, the crisp details of white ironwork stood out like lace on a valentine.

I painted it a beautiful blue the next year to match a tropical print. And the blue stayed on another season to play opposite complementary orange, red-orange, and golden orange. The terrace colors really sang that year! But the desire to try something different drove me to cover the blue paint with "sun yellow." At first my heart wasn't in it, but in the end I loved it. Every day that summer was sunny, thanks to the yellow furniture and the yellow and white flowers. But I had never attempted a completely cool color scheme, except for my tiny white garden. So during the next winter, the furniture metamorphosed into blue-green to go with the blue-pinks, mauves, and purples that I had admired in the drapery fabric.

I discovered that I liked cool, closely related hues better indoors than out and missed the happy yellows of the year before. Admittedly, finding flowers in the right shades and tints of pink was an interesting challenge, and it was fascinating to see how these colors changed, depending on the light conditions. The purples, pale pinks, and mauves looked their best on overcast days but didn't hold up well in the sun — in bright light the pastels faded and the purples appeared lifeless. Although I'm glad I tried this cool scheme, I prefer warm, bright colors in the garden.

Per Rasmussen is like me and favors strong, contrasting hues outdoors. And his preference works well under the circumstances. Pastels could never compete with the powerful sunlight that floods his terrace. "I

Jan echoes on her deck the greens of the landscape in all their infinite variety.

may not be a bright-color person indoors," he says, "but on the terrace, I really love salmon pink, yellow, and orange. There are golden orange 'Stella de' Oro' daylilies underplanted with apricot-colored pansies lining the long wall, and I always throw something blue in with them because the complementary contrast is fun. It makes your eyes jump! I also love blue for itself, and there are blue morning glories everywhere. They self-sow in the cracks between the pavers, so I transplant them. They are all over the lattice against the wall of the apartment, on the arch, even climbing up the cedar tree in the center garden. They grow into the tree and come out the top, so that in the morning it is like a blue umbrella."

Another color Per uses in abundance is white, which technically speaking is not a color at all. Nevertheless, in art, design, and the garden, it is a force to be reckoned with. White is lighter and brighter than any spectral hue and therefore commands the most attention. Its dominant character makes it a poor unifier but a perfect enhancer.

Pure white is just that, pure. It absorbs no hint or blush of any other color. Instead it reflects every color of the rainbow, equally and completely. Thus, next to white, every color appears more intensely itself. In the center garden on Per's terrace, the vivid pink and magenta impatiens and golden black-eyed Susans seem even fresher and brighter, thanks to masses of double white petunias and the light-colored fabric covering the two lounge chairs. (See pages 124, 125.)

If white is the most dominant and demanding of colors, green is the exact opposite, asking little and giving much as a background color and peacekeeper. Nature's choice for field and forest, green can be relied upon to calm a storm of clashing colors and bring a measure of compatibility to any medley of hues.

The Nickel deck and outdoor furniture at Green Dreams relate to the woodland setting in terms of color and material.

Guaranteeing harmony on the one hand, green also creates lively contrasts with hot colors such as red, yellow, and orange and reigns supreme in low-light situations. Kate Resek's garden owes a profound debt to this soothing, middle-of-the-spectrum hue. Her leafy refuge boasts a wealth of forest green in the foliage of the rhododendrons and the leaves of Virginia creeper, which covers large areas of the surrounding lattice. Only in the shade is green fully appreciated for itself.

Jan and Dave Nickels' Connecticut garden also pays tribute to nature's favorite background color. Aptly called Green Dreams, their wooded property is enclosed by verdant walls of understory shrubs beneath a ceiling of oak, birch, and tulip leaves. Taking her cue from the landscape, Jan designed a garden that fits seamlessly into its setting. She carpeted the ground on either side of narrow woodland paths with hostas, ferns, snakeroot, and other shade-loving plants. The deck and container garden are more formal extensions of the same green theme.

Furnishings

Outdoor furniture can make or break a color scheme by either blending in or standing out. While I use my wrought metal table and chairs to serve different color whims and often want it to stand out, my friend Betty Ajay strives to make garden furniture blend into nature's background hues. As a landscape designer, she has always selected low-voltage, neutral colors, such as tan, brown, or gray. "Furniture that is too bright can disrupt the unity of an entire setting," she says.

Jan and Dave Nickel wanted deck furniture that would fit into their surroundings and go with the brown siding of the house. Therefore, wood seemed a good choice, and the price was right — Dave built the

Landscape designer Betty Ajay chose charcoal gray metal furniture to harmonize with the grays of the flagstone terrace and the clapboards of her eighteenth-century house. Lighter gray fabric covers the cushions of a chair and two settees.

BELOW: This canopied chair once stood on a little stone terrace in Cincinnati overlooking the garden created by Mary Stambaugh's grandfather.

OPPOSITE: Massive wooden furniture on the patio, despite its size, diverts none of the attention from Steve's showstopping tropical border. On the contrary, the neutral gray sets off the daring flower and foliage colors.

benches and tables from salvaged lumber. With obvious satisfaction, he explains that they are made out of sugar pine "skids," which are low, wooden platforms used to ship heavy material and equipment. "I dismantle them, plane the boards, and treat them with Cuprinol, then with a clear, weatherproof stain." A good-looking lounge chair was a dump find. "Somebody was throwing it out, so I picked up the frame and made sugar pine slats for it."

Wood is an excellent, long-lasting material for garden furniture, but large-scale pieces can be clumsy in appearance and heavy to move. However, massive teak pieces are appropriate for Steve Silk's patio, which, as Steve explains, is a large area. "Or was," he adds, "before we started filling it up with plants. Anyway, we wanted the furniture to be in scale with it and were looking for a natural material that would tone in with the flagstone and go with any color scheme. We also wanted something that would be low or no maintenance. That's why we chose plantation teak. You don't have to do anything to it, and it weathers to a beautiful silver gray. The cushions are low maintenance, too, covered in a weather-resistant fabric that doesn't absorb water."

The idea of silver gray wooden furniture appealed to Per Rasmussen, too, but in the end, he decided against it. "The outdoor furniture needs to be wiped off all the time," he says, "so I went with plastic. As the gazebo, arch, and moldings are all white, I stuck with it for the sake of continuity. The focus is supposed to be on the

The rest of Mary's garden furniture is painted a soft, gray olive green to match the house.

flowers, not the furniture. I just wanted it to look clean, crisp, and kind of sparkly."

Mary Stambaugh didn't want to make a feature out of her garden furniture either. "I thought it would be better," she says, "if it just faded right in with the house." Unobtrusive in color but striking in design, Mary's garden furniture is part of her family history. She remembers summer afternoons curled up with a book beneath the canopy of her grandmother's lounge chair, the same chair that graces her garden today. "It used to be on a tiny fieldstone terrace, just off what was known as the

Long Path. Probably nobody ever sat there except my grandmother, who was a little bit eccentric."

Blessed with an interesting grandmother and a grandfather who gardened passionately until the day he died, Mary treasures mementos from their Ohio home and garden, including a wooden glider and four delicately crafted iron chairs. The chairs were manufactured by John B. Salterini, who emigrated from Italy in the 1940s and started making iron garden furniture in Brooklyn, New York.

Now painted the same soft olive green as the house,

these pieces are woven into the fabric of Mary's Connecticut life and garden. "My greatest pleasure," she says, "is to look out at the terrace and be reminded of my grandmother, my grandfather, and friends from Cincinnati and other places. It means so much to have things in your garden from other people. It keeps the life of the person who gave it to you going."

Accessories

From Objets d'Art to Water Features

By this time your container garden should be completely furnished, which, according to *Chamber's 20th Century Dictionary*, means supplied with "what is necessary." But perhaps you still yearn for some finishing touch, something unnecessary but special — a fountain, sculpture, or other decoration — that will make your terrace, deck, or rooftop unique. If so, you are in good company.

The Victorians were the first northerners to make use of the terrace for outdoor living, and they couldn't resist objets d'art, indoors or out. Their gardens were thronged with statues of demure maidens, well-fed children, dogs, and deer. While tastes have changed, gardeners haven't. We still

A bit of ingenuity and a small recirculating pump bring the sound of falling water to Steve Silk's container garden. The Vietnamese bowls remind him of his traveling days and fit into the jungle setting.

OPPOSITE: At Green Dreams, the man-made objects defer to nature. Half seen among the native understory shrubs and shade-loving perennials, a skeletal globe, reminiscent of an armillary sphere, rises out of the greenery. On either side, classical columns hold urns of fuchsia just above the foliage of the plants carpeting the woodland floor.

love ornaments, and garden centers oblige us with an array of urns, obelisks, columns, statuary, and birdbaths. The snag is that, unlike plants, these additions are permanent — at least until the next tag sale — and care should be exercised in their selection. You need to consider the size and style of the ornament in relation to the size and style of your container garden, the architecture of your house or building, and its setting.

Ornaments

If surprise and humor are your intent, some wacky found object might hit just the right note. In which case Rebecca Cole's book *Potted Gardens* will give you inspiration and permission to be adventurous and original. But if you feel uncomfortable with the idea of junkyard "finds," you might be better off using something more conservative. This is not to say that an over-the-top collection of treasures can't be incorporated into a container garden, but it is risky business unless you have a flair for decorating, a strong sense of design, and a healthy respect for the genius loci.

Jan Nickel has all three, plus ample space for the large collection of decorative objects that she has tucked about her woodland setting and among the plants on the deck. Made from wood, stone, concrete, rusted steel, or other natural materials, they don't advertise their presence but blend into the surroundings. "I would like it to seem as if the ornaments had been there forever," she says. "You should come upon them by chance."

Visitors always stop to admire the planter before leaving the deck.

OPPOSITE: In Jan Nickel's meditative "birdbath" garden, three granite balls, in perfect relation to the size and shape of their container, nestle among soft mounds of mossy selaginella and other creeping plants.

The granite turtle has occupied this shallow container for so long that lichens have formed on its hand-carved shell.

BELOW: At my back door, a pair of Mexican pottery chickens, with their flock, preside over the entryway.

OPPOSITE: From a shelter attached to the wall, a figure of Saint Francis watches over the garden and the various creatures that inhabit it.

Although Jan doesn't like garden ornaments that "bellow out at you," she has created a showstopper in what she calls the "birdbath garden." The stone planter stands alone at the exit ramp leading from the deck into the woods. The design is simple: a pedestaled bowl elevated on a square base. In the bowl, three granite balls of different sizes rest among mossy hummocks of selaginella.

"I've had that planter a long time," she says. "I don't remember where I got it, but the granite balls came from Smith and Hawken. The shape of the bowl seemed to call for something low-growing to fill in around them and drape over the edge. So I used selaginella, Scotch moss, and baby's tears. The balls add the kind of meditative look I wanted. It's supposed to make you pause before you leave the deck."

Preferences in garden decoration are highly personal. Having grown up in the country loving native flora and fauna, I am prejudiced in favor of nature themes and animal sculpture. Thus a realistically carved granite turtle caught my eye in a craft shop on Cape Cod years ago. Too small to be noticed out in the

garden, the turtle found a home on the terrace in a terra-cotta bowl, surrounded by hens-and-chicks. A fondness for chickens is another holdover from my youth, and pottery chickens go well with an old farmhouse. Every year a pair of ceramic Mexican chickens, and their ever increasing flock of hens-and-chicks, play an important role in the container garden flanking one of the entrances.

In a garden surrounded by forest and carved out of abandoned farmland, images of creatures have always seemed more appropriate than figurative sculpture. We share the terrace with birds, squirrels, chipmunks, and assorted small amphibians and reptiles. Hummingbirds, suspended in midair above the fuchsias, treat us to a blur of minute wings and iridescent plumage. Leopard frogs hop out of the flowerpots whenever I am watering. Occasionally a black and yellow striped garter snake

slithers across the cement, disappearing through one of the drain holes. This is no place for statues of chaste Victorian maidens. But the saint who called birds and beasts his brothers does belong here. With benign tolerance, a small terra-cotta figure of Saint Francis watches over his kin from a barn-siding shelter attached to the garage wall.

Steve Silk's garden ornaments are few in number but have special meaning for him. Before he became a stay-at-home father and fell in love with gardening, he was a footloose travel writer and photographer with a soft spot for tropical climates. Both the plants and the decorative objects in his container garden are remembrances of journeys past.

"My travels are now pretty much limited to the backyard," he says. "And I'm good with that, but these things are my little touchstones. A nice carved-stone temple guardian reminds me of Bali. That's a place I've been a number of times and have affection for. And because I've traveled such a lot in Southeast Asia, I wanted a Buddha."

Although Steve's wooden image of Buddha was purchased in the United States, it speaks to him of its place of origin. "I like having these reminders of past travels in the garden," he says. "In a sense, the whole tropical border is just that. Although it isn't like any landscape in nature, many of the plants are similar to plants I saw and liked growing in other countries and other climates."

Most of the man-made additions to Per Rasmussen's terrace are architectural in function and form, like the short, square columns topped with concrete pineapples that anchor the corners of the center garden. But when it comes to pure decoration, he also leans toward the Far East. A pair of Foo dogs, which traditionally stand guard over Buddhist temples, perform

Souvenirs of a traveling life bring a touch of the exotic to Steve Silk's container garden and remind him of his days as a travel writer and photographer.

LEFT: Surrounded by flowers and foliage, a temple guardian from Bali keeps a watchful eye on visitors.

BELOW: The bowl in the figure's outstretched hands holds a single flower, which is replaced every day.

OPPOSITE: One of a pair of Foo dogs that guard the herb garden on Per's terrace. These fanciful creatures play a prominent role in the Buddhist religion, protecting temples and tombs from evil spirits. The animals are often depicted with one paw raised and resting on a sphere.

this role at the entrance to the herb garden. "We have a lot of Asian things inside and wanted to put an Asian touch outdoors, too," he says.

In keeping with a house furnished in the style of the Arts and Crafts movement, Lee Anne White's deck is innocent of clutter and unadorned, except for a birdhouse that sits on the dining table. "My dad made the birdhouse," she says. "Each year on Christmas Eve, everyone in the family brings a handmade or home-

made gift. We draw numbers, and when your turn comes, you can take a wrapped package or a gift that someone else with a lower number has already selected. The birdhouse got 'stolen' several times before the gift swap was over that year. But it matches our house color and style, and although it's functional, it has never made it to a post in the garden. I decided I liked it best right here on the table."

Most of Mary Stambaugh's garden ornaments also have family associations and are useful as well as decorative. "I have all my grandmother's copper watering cans. She had eight or nine, which she used all the time, and so do I. In the winter I bring them in and put them under the sideboard in the dining room for decoration." During the growing season, one of the watering cans, now darkened with age, stands ready for use next to the little pool on Mary's gravel terrace. Nearby, a giant clam, which her grandmother acquired in

California and had shipped back to Cincinnati, arches its crenulated back among the potted plants.

Water Features

There is a place for water in every container garden, no matter what its size, shape, style, or surroundings. The sight and sound of moving water create an atmosphere of peace and tranquillity. But even still water can be mesmerizing. What you see depends on your mind-set and angle of vision. Do you just see water or do you see the reflection of sky and a world turned upside down? Wonder can be yours in a birdbath.

Moreover, a birdbath allows you to enjoy water on your deck, patio, or rooftop without electric pumps or wiring. And you will be amazed by the speed with which word gets out in avian circles. Soon birds will appear to perch on the rim and drink or, if it is shallow enough, splash vigorously in the water. In addition to the entertainment they provide, they will repay your hospitality by reducing the insect population in your container garden.

Should you want to provide water for your birds in the winter, most hardware stores carry thermostatically controlled heaters for keeping water buckets and birdbaths free of ice. Our glazed pottery birdbath, designed by potter

OPPOSITE TOP: For reasons both sentimental and aesthetic, Lee Anne White treasures the birdhouse made by her father. In style and color, it matches her house.

OPPOSITE BOTTOM: Mementos from Mary Stambaugh's Ohio youth add interest to her gravel terrace. The giant clamshell and an antique earthenware flowerpot came from her grandmother's home in Cincinnati.

BELOW: A hidden deicer keeps this glazed pottery birdbath from freezing in the winter. In cold weather it provides drinking water for the birds and is almost as popular as the feeder.

Trevor Youngberg, has a deicer concealed beneath a dome pierced with holes. This deicer is designed to keep up to fifteen gallons of water ice free, can be plugged into any grounded outdoor outlet, and uses less than two hundred watts. We are always astonished by the number of birds that come for water during the cold weather, nearly as many as visit the feeder. Birdbaths require next to no maintenance. They should be emptied, scrubbed out, and refilled with fresh water daily during the summer and occasionally in the winter.

Jan Nickel has found an easy way to incorporate water into the garden that requires no maintenance at all. She fills a handsome ceramic container with water and adds easy-to-grow aquatic plants, such as water lettuce and water hyacinths. "That's all there is to it," she says, "and it never gets algae. In the fall I just empty the container, turn it upside down, and leave it outside." Steve does something similar with a large

Lush foliage and the cooling presence of water are particularly welcome on Lee Anne White's hot, sunny Georgia deck. The trough provides a suitable home for *Colocasia esculenta* 'Illustris,' moisture-loving iris, and scouring rush (*Equisetum hyemale*).

OPPOSITE: Minute leaves of duckweed, floating in a container of water, provide contrast in size and texture with the surrounding foliage.

Ready-made fountains, like this arrangement of copper pots, come fully assembled and can be plugged into any grounded outlet.

glazed pot that he uses as decoration in the foreground of his tropical border. He simply fills the pot with water and floats duckweed on the surface. The aquatic plant's expanding mat of tiny green leaves contrasts in color, size, and texture with the foliage of nearby coleus and the large, barbed leaves of the golden fruit of the Andes (*Solanum quitoense*).

Although Lee Anne White's cattle trough water garden is much bigger than Steve's pot and Jan's ceramic container, it is no more trouble. She fills it in the spring, installs the aquatic plants in their pots, and lets nature take its course. While she admits that the water does get a bit grungy over the summer, it doesn't show. "The trough is filled and surrounded with plants," she says, "so you're not really aware of the water. It just looks like a dark-bottomed pool. And maintenance is easy. Every spring I siphon out the water, scrub down the trough, and refill it."

Falling water adds a new sensory dimension to container gardens, producing a repertoire of refreshing sounds. Ready-made fountains require no assembly and are available in many sizes and styles from catalogs and garden centers. All you have to do is plug them in. Some, like Steve's double copper pots that spill water from one to the other, are attractive to both eye and ear. "Kate saw this one somewhere and liked it," he says. "She thought it would bring a note of tranquillity to her office, but in the end I inherited it for the garden." Here it found a home among the plants in the tropical border.

Long ago I decided that our garden did not lend itself to decoration but changed my mind when our friend, artist Elizabeth MacDonald, presented us with a blue ceramic ball. Elizabeth has spent a lifetime expressing a passion for the natural world through works in clay. In the blue ball, she combines the earthy with the ethereal. While the texture recalls the rough feel of stoneware, the color brings to mind the mutable summer sky. And the shape echos that of the earth itself.

The blue ball is the perfect garden ornament. And we had the perfect place for it as the focus of an island bed in the upper lawn. Gazing at it one morning, my husband, Martin, remarked, "Wouldn't it be fun if the ball did something? Like shoot water out the top?" And so began a joint venture involving Elizabeth, Martin, and potter Trevor Youngberg.

At Martin's behest, Elizabeth made a new ball, which she provided with holes, top and bottom. Trevor adapted one of his birdbath designs to accommodate a small submersible pump purchased by Martin from Home Depot, and together they worked out the specifics of the fountain. The base would have to be made in two pieces: the bowl, modified to hold the pump and ball, and a hollow pedestal to support the bowl. Once these parts were ready, the rigid plastic

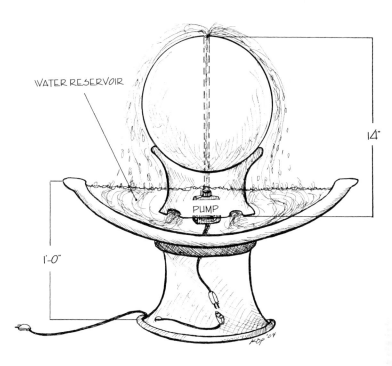

The fountain uses a small pump meant for tabletop water features and pond art. The maximum pumping height is two and one-half feet. At a height of one foot sixty gallons of water an hour is pumped through the fountain. The pump is designed to operate underwater. The water level in the reservoir must be high enough to cover the pump at all times.

A blue ceramic ball created by artist Elizabeth MacDonald serves as the focal point of an island bed.

tubing was attached to the pump outlet, conducted up through the ball and out the hole on top, and cut off flush with the surface. (See page 149.)

The completed fountain is a thing of beauty and a joy for the summer months. Water rises in a little jet from the top of the ball, spreads a glistening film over its entire surface, and quietly returns to the bowl. Although we have to strain to hear its soft whisper, the birds have no difficulty in locating the source of water. All day long, goldfinches, chipping sparrows, and other small birds stop by to drink from the bowl and duck their heads under the jet on top.

The only maintenance involved with a small fountain like mine is keeping it clean. During the summer I unplug it once a day, wipe out the bowl, and refill it. In very hot weather, the water level needs topping off once a day with the hose. In the fall I disassemble it and bring the whole thing, including the pump, inside for the winter.

We have another water feature around the corner from the container garden near the door to the breezeway. Crude in comparison to the ball fountain, this one looks like an old-fashioned hand pump. But the water pours in a steady, delightfully noisy stream out of an old faucet into a half whiskey barrel with a black plastic liner. Martin installed the pump in the base of the wooden housing, which he designed and I built in a couple of hours. Once during the summer I siphon out the water and refill it, and every spring I repaint the wooden housing with deck paint.

Like my spouse, Steve Silk is good at harnessing water and bringing its seductive music to his container garden. He has rigged a fountain from two beautiful Vietnamese bowls. "I put one up on a tree stump and the other below it to catch the water that spills from a little bamboo spout."

It is not difficult to bring the wonderful sound of water to a deck or terrace. This old-fashioned water pump was assembled in a few hours.

OPPOSITE: This small fountain, inspired by Elizabeth MacDonald's blue sculptured ball, serves as an arresting accent on the wall of my terrace.

the Nitty-Gritty

Caring for the Container Garden

The good news is that, except for watering, the on-going care of potted plants is a piece of cake. But watering is tricky. Overwatering and underwatering account for many losses. There are no precise rules about how much water to give your plants or when, but this much is certain: nature alone will not provide enough. It becomes your responsibility to bridge the gap. The following guidelines will help you determine the amount of water your plants need.

Watering

First, read the plant labels. Under "general care" you will find information about that particular plant's moisture requirements. Because I save

Colorful watering cans are as decorative as they are useful.

Dissolve water-soluble plant food in a two-gallon watering can and apply weekly.

labels until I can jot down the plant names in my garden notebook, I was able to look through those for last summer. The vast majority recommend growing annuals and tender perennials for pot culture in "moist, but not wet, well-drained soil." In other words, most plants do not like extremes. And until their roots are well established, newly potted plants are particularly sensitive. They don't want to be too dry or too wet. That being the case, try watering once a day in the morning. If the soil is still wet the next morning, refrain from watering until the surface dries out. Once the plants are growing vigorously, adjust the watering routine to suit that plant.

For tuberous begonias, the label reads: "Keep moist and avoid drying out." Daily watering would be in order for tuberous begonias. The same applies to cannas and many of the tropical plants with large leaves. In fact, it would be hard to overwater a canna, which delights in boggy conditions. But given the same amount of moisture, an agave or a cactus from the arid Southwest would eventually rot. These plants are equipped for desert conditions and need to live lean and dry.

To avoid overwatering his collection of cacti and succulents, Steve keeps them all together on a Victorian plant stand. While he waters the tropical plants daily, he visits the desert plants only once a week — if he remembers. "The great thing is that I put that little plant stand in a place where I rarely bother to go with the hose, unless the weather is exceptionally dry."

Besides the natural inclinations of your plants, there are other factors that affect the amount of water they need: the weather (the hotter the temperature, the more water the plant requires), the size of the container (a small container dries out more quickly than a large one), the material the container is made of (a porous clay pot loses moisture much faster than a nonporous plastic pot), and the light conditions and exposure of your deck, terrace, or rooftop.

Although Per Rasmussen switched from clay to plastic containers to conserve moisture, watering is still a daunting chore on his open, south-facing rooftop. Windswept, sun-drenched, and thirty stories above ground level, his container garden demands daily watering. "And if the weather is hot, I water twice a day — in the morning and again in the evening. It takes about forty-five minutes each time," he says. His white wooden planters are equipped with reservoirs, which can be topped off as needed. But the rest of the two hundred containers must be visited with the hose on a daily basis. As the only spigot is located in the

Daylilies love heat and moisture and flourish here against the sunny, south-facing wall of this apartment. They also benefit from the regular moisture provided by a built-in reservoir in their planter.

LEFT: A Victorian plant stand makes the perfect home for a collection of succulents and cacti, which require dry conditions and perfect drainage. Here, out of range of the hose, they are happy basking in full sun.

northwest corner of the terrace, this means carefully threading the hose around the three separate gardens.

Conversely, Kate Resek's garden requires a minimum of watering. Her rooftop is entirely surrounded and shaded by tall buildings. The protected site means less wind to evaporate the moisture and ensures cooler temperatures. So instead of every day, she gets away with watering every two or three days, depending on the heat and whether nature has obliged with any rainfall.

Our terrace on the north side of the house receives some shade, but I still have to water at least once a day during the height of the growing season. And Mary Stambaugh, whose terrace also faces north and is partially shaded by large maple trees, nevertheless finds herself dragging hoses around every day. Lee Anne White, on the other hand, whose deck bakes under the Georgia sun, does no watering at all. Her secret, of course, is a drip irrigation system, which you can buy in kit form for about forty dollars.

The component parts of a typical drip irrigation system include plastic tubing of different diameters, an adapter/fertilizer injector that attaches to the faucet, and a variety of small devices called emitters that actually deliver the water to the pots.

The typical kit comes with an adapter to attach to your faucet, half-inch plastic tubing for the main water line, and smaller-gauge tubing that can be cut to different lengths and run from the main artery to each container. According to Lee Anne, assembly isn't difficult, but she finds running the lengths of micro tubing to the individual containers tedious. "Especially as I tend to rearrange my pots from year to year, which can mean running new or longer lines and swapping out some lines and capping others. I can assemble the whole thing in a day," she says. "I just have to get motivated, find all the bits and pieces, and hook it up. Once that's done, there is no maintenance until it's time to put things to bed in the fall."

Steve Silk swears by his drip system. It made all the difference to his life when his son was small and he had little time to devote to the container garden. "To set it up only takes a few hours," he says. "And even a fairly elaborate system like mine is inexpensive when you consider the time it saves. When the lines are in place, all I need to do is turn on the faucet for forty-five minutes each morning, and all my pots are watered automatically. You can even leave the tubing outside all year, though I don't. I gather it up in a big tangle and take it indoors for the winter, then unravel it again in the spring."

While Lee Anne's system is hidden by the flooring of the deck, Steve runs the inconspicuous black plastic tubing on the ground behind his tropical border and, in some places, conceals the main line with mulch. "I also have it snaking up my pergola," he says, "where it serves a few hanging baskets. I'm often surprised by how unobtrusive it is once the plants begin to grow and the garden starts filling in."

As Steve has had his drip system the longest, I asked him to share his expertise. See the accompanying sidebar.

DRIP IRRIGATION

Drip irrigation systems are a lot like Tinkertoys: it's easy to snap them together as long as you've got all the pieces to build what you want. I started with a kit specifically intended for containers. It came with a variety of emitters (devices that control precisely how much water is delivered to each pot in the system) and two sizes of tubing. The smaller tubing connects to the larger with little plastic pipes, barbed at each end so they won't pull out once installed.

A customized drip irrigation system, hidden by masses of trailing foliage, provides the right amount of moisture for each plant. The banana tree in the foreground (right), the brugmansia (background far left), and the black elephant's ear and variegated canna (in front of the brugmansia) demand and receive the most water.

The kit includes a pressure-regulating gizmo and filter. The whole system must be equally pressurized to work properly, but this shouldn't present a problem unless you have very low water pressure. The regulator and filter attach to a standard outdoor faucet, and you can add a timer and/or a fertilizer injector. The filter assembly is provided to prevent blockages, which are typically caused by debris or mineral particles found in well water.

Most kits provide a selection of emitters. The two most popular sizes are those that deliver one and two gallons an hour. These are fine for the majority of my plants. But I also have very thirsty plants such as brugmansias, elephant's ears, abutilons, cannas, and others. In order to thrive, they need lots of water, much more than the one- and two-gallon emitters could deliver in a reasonable length of time. Fortunately, a trip to the garden center solved the problem. I discovered all kinds of add-on components for the system, including adjustable minisprinklers that deliver from five to ten gallons an hour.

On the whole, I use one-gallon emitters for undemanding plants in one-, two-, or three-gallon pots and two-gallon emitters for those in slightly larger pots or for plants that require more water. The really thirsty ones are treated to a custom setup, either two two-gallon emitters or a minisprinkler. And it takes two sprinklers each to satisfy my big bananas and brugmansias.

The moral of these stories is that if you have a bit of manual dexterity and don't rearrange your pots too often, drip irrigation may be your best bet. But spring is such a busy time for gardeners that many of you will probably continue to water with the hose as I do, instead of taking the time to set up a drip system. Watering takes me about half an hour every morning, and I enjoy doing it. It is a peaceful, soothing activity.

Fertilizing

Fertilizing and watering go hand in hand. Every time you water, nutrients in the soil are washed away and must be replenished in one way or another. The easiest way is by using a water-soluble all-purpose plant food. If you have summoned the will to install a drip system, you can kill two birds with one stone by purchasing the fertilizer injector, which adds the nutrients to the water.

I use Jack's Classic water-soluble plant food, which has been around for forty-five years from J. R. Peters Company. The important ingredients are 20 percent nitrogen, 20 percent phosphate, and 20 percent potash, with traces of half a dozen other elements. I apply it as directed, one tablespoon per gallon of water, once every week or ten days. Measuring the granules, filling the watering cans, and transporting them to the plants is time-consuming because you have to make

sure the water has percolated through the soil in each pot. It should drip out the bottom of the container.

The big tropical plants enjoy their weekly feedings, and by the end of July, they put on a tremendous show. But I don't treat the hardy evergreens in containers to such rich fare. They get a small handful of an organic granular fertilizer in the spring and a shot of Jack's Classic once or twice during the summer.

Per Rasmussen puts acid stakes into the pots with his evergreens in the spring and uses water-soluble plant food every couple of weeks during the season. Lee Anne White hardly uses any fertilizer, except at planting time. In the spring she incorporates slow-release pellets into the soil, and during the summer she gives the tropical plants, such as the coleus, brugmansias, and bananas, a dose of water-soluble organic fertilizer once a month.

Deadheading, Pinching Back, and Rearranging

With watering and fertilizing taken care of, the remaining chores in a container garden might be called "grooming." This entails nothing more than removing spent flowers — otherwise known as deadheading — cutting or pinching back overly long shoots to keep plants shapely, and shuffling the pots around to take advantage of their best moments.

Although I grow a good many plants — such as plectranthus, coleus, sweet potato vine, and licorice plant — for their decorative leaves, I'm a sucker for flowers and am resigned to deadheading. A quick word about this savage-sounding practice. It is actually a kindness to all flowering plants, annual and perennial, to prevent the formation of seeds by removing their faded blossoms. Producing seeds taxes the food and water supply that

would otherwise be employed in revitalizing the whole plant. Deadheading preserves these vital resources and stimulates the development of more flowers.

In his book *The Annual Garden,* Peter Loewer says, "An active thumb and forefinger can be a great gift to a garden by effectively pinching back young plants to encourage bushiness and removing spent flowers before they can go to seed." The related activities of deadheading and pinching back can certainly make the difference between a tidy, attractive container garden and a shambles. The technique is simple. Cut off withered blossoms and flowering stems. I use a pair of ARS pruners to do the job. The pruners are small, feel good in the hand, and have lethally sharp blades. You should also clean up fallen petals. Petals and spent flower heads resting on leaves eventually result in damage to the foliage.

Per Rasmussen hides flowering perennials that have passed their prime among the shrubs against the west wall of the garden, behind the tall black-eyed Susans.

OPPOSITE: With sharp pruners, shorten overly long stems, cutting them back to a pair of leaves or a side branch or pair of side branches. Here a stem of tradescantia is removed, taking it back to a new side shoot.

When the outside leaves of Steve Silk's red Abyssinian banana become tired-looking, he removes them to keep the plant tidy and to expose its gleaming trunk.

OPPOSITE: Fuchsias shed their spent flowers with abandon. However, their beauty and long season of bloom make them worth the effort of cleaning up after them.

Pinching or cutting back the growing tips of bushy plants like coleus and plectranthus fosters the development of side branches, which in turn encourages the plant to become fuller and more compact. I also shorten the long, semitrailing stems of cascading petunias, Australian fan flower, lantana, Mexican flame vine, tradescantia, and others. This clipping and nipping goes on all season.

Lee Anne does a minimum of deadheading because most of her plants are grown for their foliage. But Per has his work cut out for him with hundreds of flowering plants that cry out to have their spent blossoms removed. "I'm a fanatic about it," he says. "I deadhead every morning and vacuum the terrace almost daily to keep it neat and clean looking. But that's about it for summer maintenance, unless you count moving pots. One of the nice things about container gardening is being able to move the plants around so that when something comes into bloom, you can put it where you can see it, then tuck it out of sight when it is past its prime. I hide things that have gone by against the far west wall of the terrace at the base of shrubs and behind the tall black-eyed Susans. Having no place to store plants that have gone by, I camouflage them instead."

Steve is an inveterate mover of plants in his tropical border. "I like the plantings tightly woven, overlapping, and lush looking," he says. "As the plants grow, I move their pots farther and farther apart and away from the wall, which substantially decreases the usable space on the patio. I also raise and lower the pots. I've got some on top of a garbage can to give them height at the back of the border. By August I usually have to take in some of the furniture because space has become so tight."

Except for laying the irrigation system and shuffling pots, Steve's container garden is low maintenance. Of course, there are always new "finds" that have to be worked into the display and a few disappointing performers to be yanked out. "Otherwise," he says, "the biggest effort is cutting the lower leaves off the bananas, which I do every couple of weeks to open the view, clean up the plants, and keep them more upright looking. It also exposes their beautiful ebony-colored trunks. I slice the unwanted leaves at the base of the trunk and tear them off right at soil level so that you don't see any scarring. I also fertilize weekly, but I don't do much in the way of deadheading, as I have so much foliage."

Although maintaining a container garden requires no special tools, I recommend a pair of ARS pruners and a couple of garden totes made of tough, woven polyethylene. The totes, which are available from catalogs and garden centers, are lightweight, come in various sizes, and are invaluable for cleaning up fallen leaves and clippings. The pruners can be ordered from Charley's Greenhouse and Garden in Mount Vernon, Washington.

Per urges rooftop gardeners to purchase a dolly and/or a hand truck. "Then when you want color somewhere," he says, "you just get out the dolly and move something into position." And don't forget designer Marilyn Rennagel's little red wagon for transporting plants, pots, and bags of soil from the elevator, through the apartment, and out onto the terrace.

Finally, there is the vacuum cleaner or humble broom and dustpan. You will need them because some of our most popular container plants, such as impatiens and fuchsia, are notoriously messy. I gave up on the enchanting double impatiens because it littered the terrace daily with hundreds of rosebud flowers. The hybrid fuchsias with large pendant blossoms are almost as bad, but they are so floriferous and have such a long blooming season that I can't do without them.

CHAPTER NINE

Winding Down

Propagation, Overwintering, and Storage

Some years I wish that summer would never end, and other years it is a relief when the first frost wipes out the annuals and the tenderest of the tender perennials. Either way, as autumn draws on, container gardeners must ponder the question: To be or not to be? Whether it is nobler to overwinter difficult plants or to abandon them to their fate. Annuals have the grace to die swiftly without putting gardeners on the spot. But most of us have to fumble our way to a decision about the tender shrubs and perennials.

Depending on the plants, there are four methods of preserving tender species. You can bring them

To root cuttings in water, set them in a north-facing window where they will have light but no direct sun. Cane begonia, ivy, and plectranthus put out roots in about two or three weeks.

Rooted cuttings of tender shrubs and perennials spend the winter in a cellar under fluorescent lights.

OPPOSITE: My guest room serves as a cool greenhouse to house tender plants and cuttings.

indoors and treat them as houseplants; take cuttings and scrap the parent plants; store the dormant tubers, rhizomes, corms, and bulbs in a cool, dark place, such as the basement; or trick the plants into dormancy by putting them in cold storage with the tubers, rhizomes, corms, and bulbs and withholding light and water.

Propagating Tender Plants by Cuttings

It is easy to take cuttings. Remove a side shoot or the top few inches of a stem from the parent plant and pot up the shoot in moist peat moss, sand, potting soil, or a combination of media. Or you can root cuttings the old-fashioned way in a glass of water. I've had success with plectranthus, coleus, tradescantia, brugmansia, ivy, and cane begonia and suspect there are other plants that would also respond favorably to this simple method of propagation. However, it is a hit-or-miss technique: some plants root easily; others don't root at all.

Steve Silk's method is a bit more trouble but more reliable. "I take cuttings from the tip of a stem with three sets of leaves. After removing the lower set and any flower buds with scissors or a razor, I dip the ends of the stems into powdered rooting hormone and pot up the cuttings in a damp — not wet — peat and perlite mix, about half and half. When I've gently firmed the mix around the cuttings, they are ready to go under fluorescent lights." In a warm area of the basement, he has a tiered light system that covers about forty square feet.

To maintain a humid atmosphere for the cuttings, he puts them in a miniature greenhouse made out of a clear plastic sweater box. The lid serves as the floor, and the bottom covers the cuttings. He puts the whole thing under the lights on a heating pad, which he uses later on for starting seeds. In this favorable environment, coleus and plectranthus root in ten to fourteen days. The new plants then spend the winter either under lights in the basement or as houseplants in bright windows around the house.

A seldom-used guest room on the second floor suffices for what I do. Although the room is bright and sunny, with windows on three sides — south, west, and north — the light isn't as strong as direct sun. To boost it to a more acceptable level, my husband has erected a sort of gallows to support two four-foot-long fluorescent light fixtures, each holding a pair of wide-spectrum tubes, above a long table made from planks resting on sawhorses.

With the radiators turned off, this room makes a reasonable home for tender plants that like bright light and can tolerate temperatures as low as forty-five degrees Fahrenheit at night and between fifty-five and sixty degrees during the day. Although a range of sixty degrees at night and seventy degrees during the day is recommended for most houseplants, some actually prefer it cooler. These include abutilons — they love cool temperatures — as well as fuchsias, brugmansias, geraniums, and ivies.

I gave up taking cuttings of easily obtained plants such as coleus, plectranthus, and salvia long ago, but I have been preserving *Brugmansia* 'Charles Grimaldi' this way for fifteen years. Before the first frost, I clip off six- to ten-inch side shoots, remove any flower buds, and stick the cuttings in water. Set in the north window of the kitchen at room temperature — seventy degrees in the day, sixty degrees at night — they root in about two and a half weeks. When each cutting sports a number of vigorous-looking roots, I pot them up, using Fafard potting mix and four-inch pots. After the cuttings have been watered and allowed to drain, I let them settle for a day before moving them to the guest room. At this time it is still relatively warm outside, and the guest room temperature remains in the sixty-degree range. By the time winter sets in, the cuttings have gradually become acclimated to the cooler temperatures.

I have never been one for houseplants, but a venerable clivia, which we inherited from the previous owner of our house, gets special consideration. It spends the winter under lights in the sitting room, where the nighttime temperature only goes down to sixty degrees. Although it doesn't bloom indoors, every summer for more than forty years it has produced half a dozen or more magnificent orange flower heads, and its progeny have traveled far and wide among friends and acquaintances.

One of the red Abyssinian bananas en route to its winter home in a cool, dark part of the basement. Steve finds it worth the struggle to overwinter the whole plant rather than cut it to the soil level. The preserved plant already has a head start in the spring and will achieve greater height during the growing season.

RIGHT: In a cool, dark corner of Steve's basement, canna rhizomes, fingerlike dahlia tubers, and the round tubers of voodoo lilies rest for the winter. Behind them, bananas and brugmansias, forced into dormancy, await warmth, water, and the spring sunlight to bring them back to life.

Cold Storage of Rhizomes, Tubers, Bulbs, and Corms

Many of our most valuable and interesting container plants grow from thickened, underground, food-storing organs, which botanists call by different names, depending on their structure. Rhizomes and tubers are swollen underground stems, the difference between the two being of more interest to scientists than to gardeners. Bulbs are easier to recognize, as they are made up of fleshy scales attached to a base, like an onion. And corms come in different shapes but are solid throughout. For what it is worth, cannas, alocasias, and bananas grow from rhizomes; dahlias, caladiums, and sweet potato vines from tubers; Asiatic lilies and pineapple lilies from bulbs; and gladioli and crocosmia from corms.

As usual, I take the easy way out with tuberous and rhizomatous plants. I wait for a frost to kill the foliage, then cut them down, leave them in their pots, and store them — pots and all — in the cellar. They need darkness and temperatures between forty-five and fifty degrees. Steve works harder on their behalf. He removes the rhizomes, tubers, bulbs, or corms from their containers, knocks off the soil, and allows them to dry in the shade out of doors. Then he labels them and stores them in cardboard boxes in the cool part of his basement.

Most books recommend moist storage in damp sand or peat moss. If you use this method, check occasionally to see if any of the rhizomes, tubers, corms, or bulbs have rotted and discard those that have. If you use the dry-storage method, check to see if any appear to be shriveling up. If so, sprinkle them with a little water.

Forced Dormancy of Tender Shrubs and Perennials

Dormancy can be thrust upon a plant by withholding water and relegating it to a cool, dark place, which is the fate that befalls Steve's banana trees every year. Even before the first frost, he manhandles the huge plants into the basement, where he leaves them all winter, without light and without water. Then, in May or when the weather has warmed up and most nights are frost free, he resuscitates the bedraggled-looking plants. "They bounce back quickly," he says, "once I get them outside during the day. I still have to drag them into the garage when frost threatens. But given water, heat, sunlight, and fertilizer, they wake right up, and within a couple of weeks I've got big, handsome plants again."

Alternatively, he lets frost have its way with the banana foliage, then cuts the plant to the base and drags the pot down to the basement. He says that the plants subjected to this harsher treatment recover at the same rate but tend to be shorter and stockier than those that have been stored in their entirety.

Other plants that Steve has successfully forced into dormancy include brugmansia; glory bower (*Clerodendrum* spp.), a shrub from Africa; Cape fuchsia (*Phygelius* x *rectus*), a subtropical perennial also from Africa; agave; and New Zealand flax (*Phormium* spp.). Brugmansia, glory bower, and Cape fuchsia can be cut to the base, but the foliage of the agaves and the New Zealand flax should be left intact. Store them all in a cool, dark place, such as a basement or a frost-free garage.

Greenhouse Propagation and Storage

Mary Stambaugh is lucky enough to have a thirteen-by-fourteen-foot greenhouse in which to overwinter plants and cuttings from her container garden. "The first two years, I kept the minimum temperature around forty degrees," she says. "I always lost a lot of cuttings but assumed that the mortality rate was normal. Last year I raised the heat to sixty degrees, day and night, and we only lost five cuttings! The heat re-

ally made a tremendous difference. At a constant sixty degrees, nothing has to struggle."

Although Mary overwinters many of her tropical shrubs in the greenhouse, its main purpose is the propagation of favorite plants. For instance, she has seven or eight different varieties of scented geraniums. "I love the rose geranium best because it was one that my grandmother always grew. She used to make little net bags, which she filled with dried rose geranium and tucked behind the sofa pillows. When you sat down in the living room, all of a sudden you were enveloped in this wonderful scent."

By the end of October, Mary's greenhouse benches are crowded with trays of geraniums. "In the old days," she says, "when my grandfather and my mother made cuttings, they always said you should take a 'heel,' a small piece of the parent plant that comes away if you pull off a shoot rather than cut it off. People don't seem to do that anymore, but I still do. You can do it with clippers. You just cut away a little piece of the main stem with the shoot." She pots her cuttings in damp Fafard potting mix and sand — three parts mix to one part sand. And the humid atmosphere of her greenhouse keeps the cuttings moist. "The trick," says Mary, "is not to overwater. In soggy soil, plants rot at sixty degrees."

Jan Nickel doesn't have a greenhouse of her own, but she spirits away many of her plants to the greenhouse where she works. There her large specimens of calico plant (*Alternanthera* spp.) and Persian shield (*Strobilanthes dyerianus*) become the source of cuttings

OPPOSITE: A collection of begonias spends the winter in Mary Stambaugh's cool greenhouse, along with a few cyclamens to provide color, and trays of geranium cuttings.

that by spring will be robust new plants ready for sale to container gardeners in northern Connecticut.

Hardy Shrubs and Perennials in Winter

Per Rasmussen and Lee Anne White, who include hardy shrubs and a good many perennials in their container gardens, simply leave these plants outside in their pots. "It's nice having a few conifers and grasses in the winter," says Lee Anne. "Anything that looks interesting or that I would leave standing in the garden, I leave on the deck until spring. But some of the perennials look so ratty by the end of the growing

Protected by the roof of a shed, my collection of pottery chickens remains dry and therefore safe from winter damage.

season that I cut them down and tuck the pots in a corner so that I don't have to look at them."

Per doesn't do anything to the perennials in the fall. He feels that the plants need the protection of their spent foliage. And the only plants he brings inside are the rosemary and the jasmine. The rest have to take their chances, along with the evergreens. "I do put the roses and the lavender up against the west wall, where they get some shelter from the wind, but that's all. And watering stops as soon as the soil freezes. However, if it's a dry winter, I water whenever there is a thaw."

Winter Storage of Pots

Storing pots in the winter depends on the material of which they are made. Different materials require different handling. Jan, who buys containers for the garden center where she works, goes by what the vendors tell her about the winter hardiness of their wares. However, in any climate where freezing temperatures are the norm, it is tempting fate to leave clay pots outside full of soil. I've mentioned this before, but it's worth repeating: when damp soil freezes, it expands enough to break a terracotta pot. The same pot can safely be left outside if it has been emptied and turned upside down so that it won't collect water.

I store all my clay pots and most of the more expensive plastic ones in the cellar. But my flock of clay chickens planted with hens-and-chicks (*Sempervivum*

My container garden slips gently into the winter season, with dracaena and trailing vinca among the last of the tender plants to succumb to frost.

spp.) stays outside under cover. Although the shed where they spend the winter is open on three sides, the roof protects the containers from rain and snow. As long as the pottery stays dry, it won't crack. This means, of course, that the hens-and-chicks must remain dry too. But these tough little succulents are renowned for their ability to withstand drought and survive under adverse conditions. They live up to their botanical name — *semper* meaning "always" and *vivus*, "alive." In the spring, with a little water, they pick up right where they left off.

Containers made of cement, fiberglass, wood, and plastic can all be left outside in the winter without protection. Jan's beautiful pedestaled bowl and the three granite balls spend winters outdoors and are none the worse for it. She leaves the bowl on its pedestal and the balls in situ. "But the plants are all tender, so I take them to work," she says. "In the greenhouse, we'll rip them apart and make lots of new babies out of them."

Winding Down

Thus, the season winds down. By the time the oak leaves, among the last to fall, have begun to accumulate in the corners of the terrace, the majority of my containers have been washed and stored in the cellar. But still the dracaenas stand tall amid the vinca in the big pots on either side of the entrance to the garden. Frost rarely levels the container garden all at once. The first freeze usually knocks out the coleus. Plectranthus is made of sterner stuff. It takes another cold snap to darken its leaves. And the fuchsias, pelargoniums, angelonias, cupheas, fan flowers, and

dahlias keep right on blooming until that morning when the roof of the barn is white and frost lies heavy on the lawn.

That morning came a while ago. Now the terrace is almost empty, except for the table and chairs, the whiskey barrels and sapling trellis, the lattice arch and wooden planters on either side of it. I've drained and put away the hoses, washed and emptied the fountain and brought it indoors, and siphoned the water out of the plastic liner for the other water feature and stored it, the pump, and the pump housing in the cellar. I still have to sweep up the last leaves and bring in the plant stands.

Meanwhile, Steve, who lives an hour north of me, has already filled box after box with tubers, bulbs, and rhizomes; his cuttings are under lights, and the bananas are resting. Up on Mary Stambaugh's hilltop, it is colder than it is here. Her container garden has long since been put to bed, and the greenhouse is full. And down in the valley along the river, Alice Reisenweaver has cleaned up her patio and is busy decorating for Christmas. We are ready for winter.

With the growing season over, Alice Reisenweaver begins decorating the patio for the holiday season.

CHAPTER TEN

Afterword

The Glad New Year

If you have just put your first container garden to bed, you may be feeling a bit melancholy. But this will pass. Soon the nursery catalogs will start arriving, filled with promise and new plants, and you will experience one of the great joys of container gardening — liberation. You are free! Last year's flops are on the compost pile; the slate is clean; the sky's the limit. Once you begin perusing the offerings from catalogs that specialize in plants suitable for pot culture, you will be off and running. Instead of battling withdrawal symptoms, you will be struggling with your conscience because your wish list greatly exceeds your budget.

A visit to Logee's Greenhouses in Danielson, Connecticut, is a sure cure for winter blues. The next best thing is one of their catalogs.

Looking for something new? This smashing chartreuse elephant's ear recently burst upon the horticultural world under a variety of names, including *Xanthosoma* 'Lime Zinger' and X. 'Chartreuse Giant.'

To get you started down the path to fiscal ruin and spiritual renewal, Steve and I have compiled a list of our favorite mail-order sources of exciting plants for container gardens (see Sources of Unusual Annuals and Tender Perennials). Like all other obsessed gardeners, we are powerfully drawn to the new and unusual. Which is not to say that we are disloyal to golden oldies, but no year goes by that we don't try something out of the ordinary. And you should too — for the fun of it. While too many unfamiliar faces might not be a good idea, don't be too conservative either. After all, "Variety's the very spice of life," as the poet William Cowper said.

Tropical and Subtropical Plants

The lush, full-color catalog from Logee's Greenhouses in Danielson, Connecticut, is usually one of the first to arrive in my mailbox. Known the world over for their vast selection of tropical and subtropical plants, the Logee family continues to carry on a tradition already more than a hundred years old. In 1891 William D. Logee began selling plants raised in his own greenhouse from a little shop on North Street in Danielson. The rest is history, as every container gardener in this country knows.

Byron Martin, a grandson of the founder, is the current president and is well suited for his role by nature and nurture. He began his career at the age of five taking care of the plants in his kindergarten classroom. Having seen his mother, Joy Logee Martin, feel the soil in the greenhouse pots before watering, he would poke his fingers into the pots at school and say to his teacher, "Not yet, Miss Leach. Let them dry out first." Pretty good advice from a five-year-old, since the trick to keeping houseplants happy is to wait until the soil is dry before watering, and then to water thoroughly.

Begonias are Byron's special love, which accounts for the extensive list of interesting cultivars offered in the catalog, many of them Logee introductions. Other family favorites include scented geraniums (*Pelargonium* spp.), parlor maples (*Abutilon* spp.), and brugmansias. By this time, the name 'Charles Grimaldi' may be almost too familiar, but it is without question one of the best and most floriferous of the brugmansias. By late summer, vigorous six-foot plants boast dozens of huge trumpet flowers that turn from primrose yellow to a delicious shade of apricot over a period of two or three days. For my yellow, green, and white color scheme, I ordered the ravishing *Brugmansia* 'Cypress Gardens,' which produced snow white trumpets on a flat-topped four-foot plant. I have also grown, with great success, *B.* x *insignis* 'Pink,' similar in stature to 'Charles Grimaldi' but with flowers that open pale pink and mature to salmon.

While I have always remained loyal to brugmansia 'Charles Grimaldi,' with apricot-colored trumpets, I recently fell under the spell of ravishing white 'Cypress Gardens.'

Strictly Tropicals

Compared with Logee's Greenhouses, Stokes Tropicals is a Johnny-come-lately. Its first catalog was printed in 1996, but since then the company has grown by leaps and bounds. Because the world of tropical plants is so enormous, Stokes has chosen to specialize in only a few groups, among them bananas, cannas, clivias, euphorbias, and several others that should be of interest to container gardeners. The company promises that the information it provides in its catalog on the care and management of these plants is the truth, the whole truth, and nothing but the truth. It even claims to have "taken all the guesswork and anxiety out of starting or adding to your tropical paradise." So press on and order a catalog. I can't wait to try *Euphorbia milii* 'Short and Sweet,' which looks like a little green ball covered with small, bright red flowers.

The Newest and the Strangest in Garden-Worthy Perennials

Plant Delights Nursery in North Carolina sends out catalogs twice a year that always make gardeners salivate. I once had the pleasure of meeting owner, founder, and superplantsman Tony Avent and the misfortune of speaking *after* him at a gardening event. No audience can resist his passionate evangelism or his seductive nursery offerings, and his catalogs are snapped up in a heartbeat. The ambitious goal of his nursery is "to change the way America gardens by offering the best, the newest, and the strangest in fun, garden-worthy perennials"—among which you will find tender plants for container gardens.

If you like black elephant's ear, *Colocasia esculenta* 'Black Runner' is an outstanding new introduction.

Although hosta is Tony's plant — he is a hybridizer of note — he has never met a canna or an elephant's ear (*Colocasia*) he didn't like. So check out *Canna* 'Australia' with "deep burgundy-black foliage" and "large, shocking red flowers." And for a pastel scheme, you might consider pale pink 'Constitution' or creamy white 'Ermine.' His offerings of elephant's ear include eleven "hard-to-find" species and cultivars, all with enormous colorful leaves. There is much more, but I'm sure you get the idea.

Uncommon Tender Plants and Choice Perennials

Steve and I look forward to the arrival of another catalog from North Carolina. Owner and guiding spirit Pam Baggett of Singing Springs Nursery is a woman after my own heart. She loves changing "the set" of her container garden each year. Her enthusiasm for plants is contagious, and you will find yourself wanting to try every one she mentions. How about chocolate-toned sugar cane with leaf blades eight feet tall? That would give your container garden a lift!

All of Steve's red-leaved Abyssinian bananas came from Singing Springs Nursery. And he keeps getting more, despite the fact that they are easy to overwinter. His excuse is that "you can never have enough of a really good thing." A lot of his coleus also came from Pam. 'New Hurricane' was "a standout," with deeply toothed red leaves edged with yellow, and also 'Oxblood,' which has "almost glowing reddish brown leaves outlined with a narrow gold margin." Thanks to the current popularity of this multihued foliage plant, you might be able to get what you want at a local nursery, but you would be hard put to find nine species and

Red Abyssinian bananas are among Steve Silk's favorite container plants.

cultivars of cigar plant (*Cuphea*) anywhere except at Singing Springs.

I became an admirer of the genus *Cuphea* after growing *C. ignea* 'David Verity,' a big bushy plant, three feet by three feet with willowy dark green foliage and countless little red-orange tubular flowers tipped with black and white. Presumably the black suggests the burned end of a cigar and the touch of white indicates ash, hence the common name, cigar plant. It won my wholehearted approval that first summer with its nonstop flower production and perfect manners — there is no shower of spent blossoms all over the terrace from a cigar plant.

This year I tried *C. laevis* and found it just as vigorous and floriferous. The flowers, which appear at the tips of the stems and in every leaf axil, have deep pink tubes ending in tiny violet petals that stick out like ears. In her description of this species, Pam Baggett writes: "When we send you *C. laevis*, it will likely be in bloom, and without a doubt, it will still be flowering when your garden goes dormant in the fall." It was perfectly true. The bushy two-by-two-foot plant bloomed right into November.

Rare, Unusual, and Uncommon Plants

Kathy Tracey and her husband, Chris, of Avant Gardens in Dartmouth, Massachusetts, do it all: hardy

ABOVE AND LEFT: Outstanding foliage plants available at Avant Gardens include Persian shield, with iridescent purple and green foliage, and variegated shell ginger, which has large, gleaming green leaves liberally streaked with bright yellow.

OPPOSITE: Multitudes of tiny orange tubular flowers and its neat, bushy habit make the cigar plant a splendid supporting player in the container garden (foreground).

Steve Silk has high praise for the glowing red foliage of the tropical smokebush, which he first encountered at Blue Meadow Farm in Massachusetts.

and tender perennials, annuals, alpines, trees, and shrubs. And they do it well. I first met Kathy at the New York Botanical Garden, Bronx, New York, where we were cospeakers in a series entitled "American Gardening: Adoring the Exotic, Treasuring the Native." I was thrilled by her lecture, "Tender and Dramatic," and by her creative container garden schemes.

Although Avant Gardens is a mom-and-pop organization and the Traceys propagate everything they sell, they manage to offer an astonishing variety of plants. Their listing of annuals and tender perennials alone is impressive: twenty-nine unusual geraniums (*Pelargonium*), many with variegated or tricolor leaves; two dozen different salvias; half a dozen color forms of trailing sweet potato vine; and many other interesting foliage plants, such as exotic purple and green Persian shield (*Strobilanthes dyerianus*), variegated shell ginger (*Alpinia zerumbet* 'Variegata'), with striking green and yellow striped leaves, and ivies by the dozen.

One of the secrets of the Traceys' success, besides hard work and good taste, may be that they made a conscious decision to remain small, selective, and adventurous. "We do grow a tremendous variety of plants (many we don't even list), but [we] do not propagate them in great quantities." They concede that this may not be the road to riches, but they find it more exciting than mass production, and so do their customers.

Rare Plants and Garden Art

Glasshouse Works in Stewart, Ohio, is as large as Avant Gardens is small. What started thirty years ago as a modest nursery of rare plants has grown into a complex of buildings and gardens that houses more than ten thousand species, cultivars, and hybrids of uncommon plants, with a distinct nod to the tropicals. The plant listings are so comprehensive that I wouldn't know where to begin naming them. Suffice it to say that you will find all the inspiration and information you can possibly absorb in its catalog or on its Web site, found in "Sources" at the back of this book.

At the Glasshouse Works nursery, you can enjoy the tender species under glass in a conservatory or tour the outdoor gardens. There are container displays, rockeries, perennial gardens, bamboo stands, and pond areas. You will find examples of garden art throughout, another specialty of the establishment. If you go there, don't worry about getting lost en route. The grounds are so extensive and the buildings so numerous that if you take a wrong turn in the village of Stewart, you'll wind up at Glasshouse Works anyway.

Cash-and-Carry in Southern New England

Finally, if you happen to be wandering the back roads of central Massachusetts, you will not want to miss one of Steve's favorite haunts. Blue Meadow Farm in Montague Center, near Greenfield, is not a mail-order nursery, but the catalog produced by owners and founders Alice and Brian McGowan is first-rate, with excellent descriptions of the plants. There are no shiny color photographs because in order to buy plants, you have to appear in person. So go and feast your eyes on all their begonias, cannas, coleuses, and euphorbias — the McGowans have a real weakness for these genera.

One of Steve's discoveries at this exceptional nursery was the tropical smokebush, *Euphorbia cotinifolia,*

which he describes in very nearly purple prose: "When the plant is backlit, the leaves glow like smoldering rubies." Coming down to earth, he adds that it is "an indispensable hue in combinations involving orange."

You will also find many different kinds of vines — including a wide selection of morning glories and morning glory relations — which are so useful for covering trellises and arches and creating "room dividers." In addition, Blue Meadow Farm carries a great variety of trailing plants to sprawl, drape, cascade, and creep down the sides of pots and across the surface of a patio.

Last but not least, Claire's in Patterson, New York, just over the Connecticut border, carries an excellent and extensive selection of home-grown annuals and tender perennials, as well as hardy perennials, roses, and heirloom and specialty shrubs. Owner Glen Waruch is a greenhouse man from way back. He was studying forestry at college when he happened to sign up for the greenhouse propagating course as an elective. It changed his life. "My first project," he remembers, "was to do fuchsias from cuttings. Right away, I fell in love with fuchsias, and from the minute I put a knife on the first cutting, I knew what I wanted to do. I've been propagating ever since."

I hope by this time that you are feeling cheered up at the thought of next year and all the goodies awaiting you in these and so many other nursery catalogs. There's a banquet out there, only a phone call and a few dollars away. And once the catalogs begin coming, you will never be sad again to see the end of a season. Instead, you will look forward to putting the garden to bed. By December, when the catalogs start arriving, you will be eager to get through the holidays so that you can begin scheming and dreaming about your summer garden. Steve and I will be thinking of you. Good luck and happy gardening.

BASIC PLANTS FOR THE CONTAINER GARDEN

Dwarf Conifers and Broadleaf Evergreens

Andromeda / *Pieris japonica* / Zones 5 and 6

Arborvitae / *Thuja occidentalis* / Zones 3–7
    Cultivars with conical forms: 'Degroot's Spire,' 'Smaragd (also called 'Emerald Green')
    Cultivars with round forms: 'Little Gem,' 'Little Giant'

Boxwood / *Buxus microphylla* 'Tide Hill' / Zones 6–9

Bristlecone pine / *Pinus aristata* / Zones 4–7

Common juniper / *Juniperus communis* / Zones 2–6

Cultivars: 'Pencil Point,' 'Gold Cone'

Creeping juniper / *Juniperus horizontalis* / Zones 4–9
    Cultivars: 'Wiltonii,' 'Mother Lode'

Dwarf Alberta spruce / *Picea glauca* Conica' / Zone 4
    Other dwarf spruce cultivars: *P. glauca* 'Little Globe,' *P. pungens* 'Fat Albert,' 'Iseli Fastigiate'

Evergreen azalea / *Rhododendron* spp. / Zones 6–7
    Cultivars: 'Gumpo Pink,' 'Hino-Crimson,' 'Sir Robert,' 'Delaware Valley White'

Japgarden juniper / *Juniperus procumbens* 'Nana' / Zones 4–8

Miniature mountain laurel / *Kalmia latifolia* / Zones 4–9
    Cultivars: 'Little Linda,' 'Elf,' 'Tinkerbell,' 'Tiddlywinks'

Mugo pine / *Pinus mugo* / Zones 4–8

Rhododendron Yaku hybrids / *Rhododendron yakushimanum* / Zones 5b–7
    Cultivars: 'Yaku Princess,' 'Yaku Prince,' 'Yaku King'

Small Deciduous Trees

Chinese witch hazel / *Hamamelis mollis* / Zones 5–8

Crab apple / *Malus* spp. / Zones 4–7
    Species and cultivars: *Malus sargentii*, 'Red Jade,' 'Louisa'

Dwarf threadleaf Japanese maples / *Acer palmatum dissectum* / Zones 5b–8
    Cultivars: 'Crimson Queen,' 'Viridis'

Serviceberry, or shadbush / *Amelanchier canadensis* / Zones 3–7

Witch hazel hybrids / *Hamamelis* x *intermedia* / Zones 5–8
    Cultivars: 'Arnold Promise,' 'Diane,' 'Jelena' (also called 'Copper Beauty')

Ornamental Grasses and Other Hardy Perennials

Alumroot / *Heuchera* spp. / Zones 4–10

Black-eyed Susan / *Rudbeckia fulgida sullivantii* 'Goldsturm' / Zones 4–10

Blue oat grass / *Helictotrichon sempervirens* / Zones 4–8

Boltonia / *Boltonia asteroides* 'Snowbank' / Zones 4–9

Chives / *Allium schoenoprasum* / Zones 3–10

Coreopsis / *Coreopsis* spp. / Zones 3–10
    Cultivars: *Coreopsis verticillata* 'Moonbeam,' 'Zagreb'

Daylily cultivars / *Hemerocallis* x *hybrida* / Zones 3–10

English lavender / *Lavandula angustifolia* / Zones 5–8
Feather reed grass / *Calamagrostis* x *acutiflora* 'Stricta' / Zones 5–9

False dragonhead / *Physostegia virginiana* / Zones 3–10

Feather reed grass / *Calamagrotis* x *acutiflora* / 'Stricta' / zones 5–9

Fishpole, or Golden, Bamboo / *Phyllostachys aurea* / Zones 7 and 8

Fountain grass / *Pennisetum alopecuroides* / Zones 4–9

Japanese forest grass / *Hakonechloa macra* 'Aureola' / Zones 6–9

Lilyturf / *Liriope muscari* / Zones 5–10

Midcentury hybrid lily or Asiatic hybrid lily / *Lilium* spp. / Zones 3–9
   Cultivars: 'Enchantment,' 'Croesus,' 'Cinnabar'

Miscanthus / *Miscanthus sinensis* 'Morning Light' / Zones 4–9

Pygmy bamboo / *Pleioblastus pygmaeus* / Zones 7 and 8

Ribbon grass / *Phalaris arundi-nacea* 'Picta' / Zones 4–8

Sage / *Salvia officinalis* / Zones 4–10

Sea pink / *Armeria caespitosa* / Zones 3–10

Tansy / *Tanacetum vulgare* / Zones 3–9

Thyme / *Thymus vulgaris* / Zones 3–9

Tender Perennials and Annuals

Angelonia / *Angelonia angustifolia* / Zones 9–10

Australian fan flower / *Scaevola aemula* / Zone 10

Begonia / *Begonia* spp. / Zones 9–10
   Species: wax begonia: *Begonia Semperflorens-Cultorum* hybrids; tuberous begonia: *B. Tuberhybrida* hybrids; *B. Rex Cultorum* hybrids

Caladium / *Caladium x hortulanum* / Zones 9–10

Canary creeper / *Tropaeolum peregrinum* / Zones 9–10

Canna / *Canna* x *generalis* / Zones 8–11
   Cultivars: 'Tropicanna' (also known as 'Phaison'), 'Bengal Tiger' (also called 'Pretoria'), 'Pink Sunburst,' 'Intrigue'

Coleus, or painted nettle / *Solenostemon scutellarioides* / Zones 10–11

Crimson fountain grass / *Pennisetum setaceum* 'Rubrum' / Zones 8 and 9

Cup-and-saucer vine, or monastery bells / *Cobaea scandens* / Zones 9–10
   Cultivar: 'Key Lime'

Dahlia / *Dahlia* spp. / Zones 8–11

Dracaena / *Cordyline indivisa* / Zones 9–11

Fuchsia / *Fuchsia triphylla* 'Gartenmeister Bonstedt' / Zones 9–11

Geranium / *Pelargonium* x *hortorum* / Zones 9–11
   Cultivars: 'A Happy Thought,' 'Crystal Palace Gem'

Impatiens / *Impatiens* spp. / Zone 10
   Species: garden impatiens: *Impatiens walleriana;* New Guinea impatiens hybrids: *I. hawkeri*

Lantana / *Lantana camara* / Zones 10–11

Marigold / *Tagetes* spp. / annual
   Species and cultivars: French marigold: *T. patula*: signet marigold: *T. tenuifolia* 'Lemon Gem' (Gem series)

Million bells / *Callibrachoa* / Zones 7–10

Morning glory / *Ipomoea* spp. / Zones 8–10
   Species and cultivars: *I. tricolor* 'Heavenly Blue'; *I. batatas* 'Blackie,' 'Pink Frost,' 'Ace of Spades,' 'Margarita'

New Zealand flax / *Phormium tenax* / Zones 9–11

Parlor maple / *Abutilon* spp. / Zones 8–10
   Species and cultivars: *A. pictum* 'Thompsonii,' *A. megapotamicum* 'Variegatum,' 'Bartley Schwartz'

Petunia / *Petunia* x *hybrida* / Zones 7–10
   Species: *P. integrifolia*

Red Abyssinian banana / *Ensete ventricosum* 'Maurelii' / Zones 9–11

Scarlet runner bean / *Phaseolus coccineus* / Zones 10–11

Sweet potato vine

Tobacco plant / *Nicotiana* x *sanderae* / Zones 7–10
   Species: *N. alata*

Zinnia / *Zinnia angustifolia* / annual
   Cultivars: 'Crystal White,' 'Profusion Cherry,' 'Profusion Orange'

RECOMMENDED READING

A Basic and Indispensable Reference for Container Gardeners

The City Gardener's Handbook, by Linda Yang (North Adams, MA: Storey Books, 2002). Originally published as *The City Gardener's Handbook* in 1990 and subsequently as *The City and Town Gardener* in 1995, both earlier editions by Random House, New York.

This book has been the bible for urban gardeners since it was published in 1990 under its present title. Linda Yang, former garden columnist for the *New York Times,* not only writes like a dream but is truly the voice of experience when it comes to any kind of city gardening. The chapter entitled "Narrowing the Choices: Some City Plants I've Known" is a must for all urbanites. Having gardened on a balcony, on a rooftop, and in a city backyard, Yang addresses problems that arise for small-space gardeners. Her insights will be especially helpful to all-season container gardeners, whether they garden in the city, suburbs, or country.

Plants for Container Gardens

Hot Plants for Cool Climates, by Susan A. Roth and Dennis Schrader (Boston: Houghton Mifflin, 2000).

Catering to a new gardening trend, Susan Roth and Dennis Schrader collaborated on a wonderful book about growing exotic, warm-climate perennials, shrubs, and trees in northern gardens, in the ground and in containers. Roth has a degree in horticulture and botany from Cornell University and Schrader is a nurseryman, landscape designer, and passionate plantsman. The book is excellent throughout, with a useful section covering the winter treatment of tropicals and subtropicals and a splendid encyclopedia of plants that provides interesting ideas for summer containers.

The Outdoor Potted Bulb and *The Indoor Potted Bulb,* both by Rob Proctor, with photographs by Lauren Springer and Rob Proctor (New York: Simon and Schuster, 1993).

These two small but choice books offer imaginative ways of using tender and hardy bulbs in containers, along with growing tips and how-to information for the preservation of bulbs, corms, tubers, and rhizomes from year to year.

The Annual Garden: Flowers, Foliage, Fruits and Grasses for One Summer Season, by Peter Loewer (Emmaus, PA: Rodale Press, 1988).

Out of print but available and worth looking for, *The Annual Garden* describes a grand variety of plants that provide a bold show for the summer season. The full-color photographs are collected together in the middle of the book, and there are excellent black-and-white illustrations accompanying each entry. All the plants included can be treated as annuals, though some are perennial in their natural habitats.

Annuals with Style, by Michael A. Ruggiero and Tom Christopher (Newtown, CT: Taunton Press, 2000).

Your gardening library can't be without this classy, colorful, eminently reliable book on annuals (and those tender perennials we in cool climates refer to as annuals). Author Michael Ruggiero began gardening at the New York Botanical Garden at sixteen years old and, until his recent retirement, gardened and taught there for his entire professional career. Fittingly, coauthor Tom Christopher, a scholar-turned-gardener and garden writer, was a product of the New York Botanical Garden School of Professional Horticulture. Although the book deals chiefly with annuals in the garden, there is an excellent, imaginative chapter on containers.

Ornamental Grasses for Containers

Ornamental Grasses: The Amber Ornamental Grasses: The Amber Wave, by Carole Ottesen (New York: McGraw-Hill, 1989). Paperback edition, 1995.

Available on the Internet but often out of stock, this book is the hands-down best yet written on the uses and culture of ornamental grasses, and it makes fascinating reading into the bargain. Container gardeners will find a wonderful chapter entitled "Grasses for Specialized Garden Use," which includes those best suited to pot culture.

Rock Garden Plants for Containers

Rock Gardening: A Guide to Growing Alpines and Wildflowers in American Gardens, by H. Lincoln Foster, with drawings by Laura Louise Foster (New York: Crown Publishers, Bonanza Books, 1957).

Scholarly, entertaining, erudite H. Lincoln Foster was the father of American rock gardening, and his book remains a classic. The plant encyclopedia, which has detailed and enchanting descriptions of each plant, covers the cultivation of alpines and woodlanders for American gardens. A section on the construction, planting, and care of simulated stone troughs will be of interest to container gardeners and might set them off on a new hobby — creating miniature rock gardens.

A Novel Approach to Container Gardening

Potted Gardens, by Rebecca Cole, with photographs by Richard Felber (New York: Clarkson Potter Publishers, 1997).

This engaging little book is written by a former thespian. While the erstwhile actress attributes her love of gardening to her grandfather and his hired hand, there is nothing homespun about the lively text and chic design ideas you will find in *Potted Gardens.*

General Container Gardening

The Container Garden, by Nigel Colborn (London: Conran Octopus, 1990).

British garden writer Nigel Colborn is a regular judge for the Royal Horticultural Society and a frequent contributor to British gardening publications, and his fine book is intended for use on his side of the Atlantic. However, it is so good that American container gardeners should peruse it closely for design ideas and plant combinations.

The Book of Container Gardening, by Malcolm Hillier (London: Dorling Kindersley, 1991).

Another excellent British book, this one is chiefly devoted to seasonal compositions in a single container, showing readers how to assemble beautiful plant associations in different types of pots, urns, window boxes, and hanging baskets. Again, the British climate being different from most climates in the United States, make sure the four-season plants mentioned are suitable for your zone.

SOURCES OF UNUSUAL ANNUALS AND TENDER PERENNIALS

Aloha Tropicals
1247 Browning Court
2210 Bautista Rd.
Vista, CA 92083-4759
Phone: 760-941-0920
Fax: 760-941-0920
www.alohatropicals.com

Avant Gardens
710 High Hill Rd.
North Dartmouth, MA 02747
Phone: 508-998-8819

The Banana Tree, Inc.
715 Northampton St.
Easton, PA 18042
Phone: 610-253-9589

*Blue Meadow Farm
184 Meadow Rd.
Montague Center, MA 01351
Phone: 413-367-2392
Fax: 413-367-0116

Brent and Becky's Bulbs
7463 Heath Trail
Gloucester, VA 23061
Phone: 804-693-3966
Fax: 804-693-9436
www.brentandbeckysbulbs.com

Brudy's Exotics
P. O. Box 820874
Houston, TX 77282-0874
Phone: 713-946-9557
Fax: 713-960-8887
www.brudys-exotics.com

*Claire's
Haviland Hollow Rd.
Patterson, NY 12563
Phone: 845-878-6632

Dutch Gardens
144 Intervale Rd.
Burlington, VT 05401
Phone: 888-821-0448
Fax: 800-551-6712
www.dutchgardens.com

Kelly's Plant World
10266 E. Princeton
Sanger, CA 93657
Phone: 209-294-7676

Glasshouse Works
Church St.
Stewart, OH 45778
Phone: 800-837-2142
www.glasshouseworks.com

Logee's Greenhouses
141 North St.
Danielson, CT 06239
Phone: 888-330-8038
Fax: 888-774-9932
www.logees.com

Neon Palm Nursery
3525 Stony Point Rd.
Santa Rosa, CA 95407
Phone: 707-585-8100

Old House Gardens
536 Third St.
Ann Arbor, MI 48103
Phone: 734-995-1486
Fax: 734-995-1687
www.oldhousegardens.com

Pacific Tropical Gardens
P. O. Box 1511
Keau'au, HI 96749-1511
Phone: 808-936-1441
Fax: 808-966-8490
www.pctgardens.com

Park Seed
1 Parkton Ave.
Greenwood, SC 29647-0001
Phone: 800-845-3369
Fax: 864-941-4502
www.parkseed.com

Plant Delights Nursery
9241 Sauls Rd.
Raleigh, NC 27603
Phone: 919-772-4794
www.plantdelights.com

Select Seeds
180 Stickney Hill Rd.
Union, CT 06076
Phone: 800-684-0395
www.selectseeds.com

Singing Springs Nursery
8802 Wilkerson Rd.
Cedar Grove, NC 27231
Phone: 919-732-9403
Fax: 919-732-6336
www.singingsprings
nursery.com

Stokes Tropicals
P. O. Box 9869
4806 E. Old Spanish Trail
New Iberia, LA 70562-9868
Phone: 800-624-9706
Fax: 318-365-6991
www.stokestropicals.com

Swan Island Dahlias
P. O. Box 700
Canby, OR 97013
Phone: 503-266-7711
www.dahlias.com

Tropiflora
3530 Tallevast Rd.
Sarasota, FL 34243
Phone: 800-613-7520
Fax: 941-351-6985
www.tropiflora.com

Van Bourgondien Bros.
245 Route 109
P. O. Box 1000
Babylon, NY 11702-9004
Phone: 800-622-9997
Fax: 516-669-1228
www.dutchbulbs.com

Wayside Gardens
1 Garden Lane
Hodges, SC 29695-0001
Phone: 800-845-1124
www.waysidegardens.com

White Flower Farm
P. O. Box 50
Route 63
Litchfield, CT 06759-0050
Phone: 800-503-9624
Fax: 860-496-1418
www.whiteflowerfarm.com

Weird Dude's Plant Zoo
1164 Frog Pond Rd.
Staunton, VA 24401
Phone: 540-886-6364
Fax: 540-886-2223
www.weirddudesplantzoo.com

Yucca Do Nursery
P. O. Box 907
Hempstead, TX 77445
Phone: 979-826-4580
Fax: 979-826-4571
www.yuccado.com

*Denotes cash-and-carry, no mail order

USDA PLANT HARDINESS
ZONE MAP

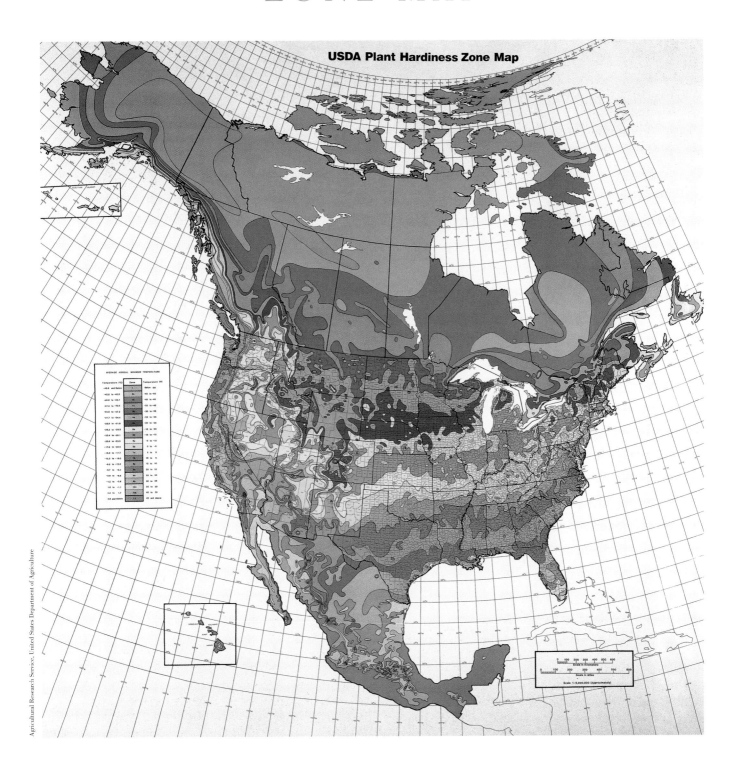

Agricultural Research Service, United States Department of Agriculture

ACKNOWLEDGMENTS

It goes without saying that Steve Silk and I are boundlessly grateful to the six gardeners who participated in the making of this book and to the other gardeners who permitted us to photograph their gardens. We are often dependent on the kindness of strangers and the help of friends. Thank you, one and all.

In addition to my best gardening buddy, Mary Stambaugh, about whom I have written before, I would like to thank Per Rasmussen, Alice Reisenweaver, Jan Nickel, Kate Resek, and Lee Anne White, former editor of *Fine Gardening*, whose handsome photographs of her own garden grace the pages of this book. Other old friends who have been generous with their time and talent include designer Marilyn Rennagel and graphic artist Kim Proctor. Special thanks to horticulturist Gregory Piotrowski. Greg's expertise has made *Gardens to Go* and the books that came before it better and more accurate. I would also like to mention the kindness of Linda Yang, author of *The City Gardener's Handbook*, who helped me understand the particular problems and pleasures of urban gardening and who introduced me to her client Kate Resek.

A seventeen-year association with *Fine Gardening* magazine has brought me interesting work, fast friends, and, most recently, a perfect partner, Steve Silk. His superb photographs now illustrate two of my books. Thanks also to the present editor of the magazine, Todd Meier, who gave us permission to use images that first appeared in *Fine Gardening*.

Finally, *Gardens to Go* and its author are more than grateful to a wonderful editor, Kristen Schilo; a designer who truly captured the spirit of the book, Kay Schuckhart; the best of all possible agents, Jane Dystel; and, on the home front, an incredibly patient, tolerant spouse, who does the grocery shopping. Many, many thanks!

— Sydney Eddison

My affection for gardening took root at home, and I'm grateful for the support I receive there for both making and photographing gardens. First, a thank-you to my wife, Kate Emery, whose artistry inspires me to create scenes worthy of her paints and canvas. I'm grateful to my son, David, whose keen fascination with the natural world never fails to reinvigorate my own sense of wonder.

My thanks to all the gardeners represented in these pages, for the inspiration their labors provide, and for their willingness to share them. I'd also like to express my gratitude to several gardeners who allowed me to photograph their gardens in preparation for this book but whose names have not been mentioned, at least until now. I'm grateful t Susan Sawicki, Chrissie D'Esopo, the late Verle Lessig, and Gary Keim, and to Chanticleer, the Wayne, Pennsylvani pleasure garden where great ideas are always on display.

I'd like to thank *Fine Gardening* magazine for introducing me to the world of horticulture — both its art and its cra My tenure as an editor there led me to some of the country's best gardeners and fostered my passion for photographi the ephemeral glories they created. My work at the magazine also led me to the door of Sydney Eddison, who since ha become a friend and mentor. Her passion for pots inspired my own, so it seems fitting that we set off together on the colorful journey that led to this book.

— Steve Silk